"This cover-your-bases, behind-the-scenes, stress-reducing book offers all you need to know and do before an interview. Marcia Ballinger uses her deep expertise as an executive recruiter to allay your fears, put you in your best light, and prepare you thoroughly for your executive interview. Before you head out your door, spend time with this book - you'll be glad you did."

— **SANDRA KREBS HIRSH,** international consultant and co-author of more than 20 publications including *LifeTypes, Discover Who You Are,* and *Introduction to Type® in Organizations* (more than one million sold)

WINNING THE EXECUTIVE INTERVIEW

MARCIA BALLINGER, PhD

with Kevin Johnson

Published by Career Innovations Press.
www.20mnm.com

ISBN-13: 978-0-9859106-6-2

To my husband Brad and our daughter Analisa

To my co-founder, Lars Leafblad, along with the incredible executive search professionals who have been my partners and colleagues over the years

SPECIAL THANKS

to Karen Kodzik, founder of Cultivating Careers, Inc.

When you really need the straight scoop, you go to a pro. Karen Kodzik, founder of Cultivating Careers, Inc. supported this book by giving me hours of insights, ideas, examples and stories.

Karen's firm, Cultivating Careers provides expert coaching and transition consulting for professionals at various stages in their careers. She is highly regarded in the Twin Cities market as contributor and source for the Minneapolis, St. Paul media on job market trends, employment and career related topics.

The author of the book *Navigating Through Now What?* a valuable resource for anyone at a career crossroad, Karen not only gave me helpful material for this book, but also some necessary but friendly encouragement along the way.

I consider Karen to be that well-rounded consultant, fellow author, business leader and friend who made it possible to complete this book. Thank you!!

www.cultivatingcareers.com

WINNING THE EXECUTIVE INTERVIEW

PART 3: APPENDIX

AT-HAND INTERVIEW WORKSHEETS

INTRODUCTION

I'M AN EXECUTIVE RECRUITER WITH MORE THAN 20 YEARS IN MY LINE OF WORK. Along with my colleagues at our firm, Ballinger|Leafblad, I assist client organizations by finding and recruiting top talent for their hard-to-fill executive positions. As a result, I'm involved with interviews all the time.

My colleagues and I have two primary perspectives on executive interviews. First, we interview executive candidates ourselves. Individuals who appear to have the right qualifications and who are interested in a client's opportunity meet with us in person, a mandatory interview before we decide to represent that individual to our client. Usually these meetings take place in our office. Sometimes I conduct them at convenient midpoints, such as restaurants. But they can take place anywhere. I once interviewed a candidate at a picnic table in a state park on a chilly, windy day!

Second, my colleagues and I sit in on interviews between our clients and our candidates. When my clients (usually a CEO or a board of directors or a selection committee) talk with individual candidates, I sit in the back of the room and observe. I don't ask questions or otherwise actively participate in the interviews. But I'm there to make introductions, kick off the meeting, and then find a spot in the back and watch. After each interview, I also debrief with the interviewer(s).

This practice isn't common among executive search firms, but I find it incredibly helpful. I'm not there to spy on individual candidates or to evaluate the interviewing skills of client organizations. Rather, my purpose is to get a second look at the candidates. I see them in another context. I watch how they interact with members of the client organization, one of whom is likely the hiring boss. As a result, I'm able to give better counsel to my clients throughout the process.

During my years in executive recruiting, I've personally interviewed more than 4,000 candidates myself and have observed well over 1,000 client interviews. Even to me, those numbers are surprising.

What I've gained through that experience is a clear sense of what works in interviews and what does not. I notice who gets invited back for further interviews and who does not. I receive feedback from clients about whom they liked and whom they did not. I see who is ultimately selected and who isn't.

I've also observed that the differences between successful and unsuccessful interviews are both obvious and subtle. This book is a collection of the knowledge I've gained from conducting and observing interviews "from the other side of the desk."

My goal is to pull back the curtain on the interview process and tell you what's really going on. Whoever you are and whatever your field, I promise to give you the best of my insights to help you succeed at interviewing and land the job you want.

PART 1

WHAT'S REALLY GOING ON

CHAPTER 1

WINNING THE INTERVIEW

PETRA BEGAY TURNED ON HER COMPUTER. TIME TO CHECK MESSAGES—AGAIN—IN HOPES OF SEEING A JOB OFFER from Byhram Nash, Inc. The hiring executive had told her the job offer would arrive "in the next few days." That was four days ago!

Petra sipped her coffee, reflecting back on the interview process. The job seemed like it could be her next great career challenge. She liked the people she'd met. And it had felt good to finish the week talking to Byhram Nash's VP of human resources. Murray Wallace had answered her questions about the company's benefits package. Now she just needed the formal offer!

Petra logged in. There it was. Right at the top. Subject line: Offer letter attached for Petra Begay.

Petra opened the document. It was a formal letter extending an offer of employment as vice president of sales and marketing at Byhram Nash, reporting to the chief executive officer, starting in two weeks, and on and on.

Generally, Petra felt excitement, gratitude, and relief. This was a job that felt right. During the last several weeks, and over the course of the interviews, she had become more and more connected to the company's mission, direction, and people.

She noticed a possible small discrepancy between the bonus compensation amount listed in the offer letter and her understanding of the bonus plan at the vice president level at Byhram Nash. She shrugged. A quick call to Murray or her new boss should clear that up. She wasn't going to make a big deal out of a small percentage difference. But she wasn't going to let it go either.

"I got it!" she yelled. Petra's spouse wasn't at home, but her dog was. Mo, their dachshund, looked up from his dog bed in the corner. "I'm the new vice president of sales and marketing at Byhram Nash!"

CHAPTER 2

WHY YOU NEED THIS BOOK

YEARS AGO I TOOK PART IN A COMMENCEMENT where I sat in the front row on stage. The event speaker was Captain Mark Kelly, naval aviator and astronaut. When he stepped to the podium in front of many hundreds of people, he talked about his participation in U.S. Naval Test Pilot School, and a wartime incident in which he had accidently flown into enemy air space. He also told of his multiple travels in space, including four as pilot or commander of the space shuttle. Captain Kelly stood only a few feet away from me. As he reached to turn a page in his notes, I noticed his hand quivering. There'd been no sign of shaking earlier that day during our conversation over lunch, and I couldn't help but conclude that he felt a bit nervous. And why not? Even though he had circled the earth over 600 times, at that point in his career he seldom gave presentations. Here he was, up on stage, in a strange setting, talking to an unfamiliar audience.

In a similar way, amazingly capable people with years of career success can become anxious in an interview.

Interviews can be tough, stressful. Why? Well, you don't look for a new job every day. You might apply for jobs only half a dozen times in your serious adult career.

On top of that, the interview setting is often uncomfortable, or worse. You find your way to a location you probably don't know, walk through a strange lobby, and perhaps meet in a cold conference room or a sterile office. You're engulfed in unfamiliar surroundings. Most likely, you're meeting with people you don't know well—or at all. Who are they? What's the pace and style of their conversation? What cultural cues might you miss?

The interview itself might make you feel uncomfortable. Will the questions be difficult? What topics do you hope to avoid? How will you know if you're making a good impression? How long will the process last?

It's no wonder people get nervous about interviews! Even high-ranking executives get interview jitters. **Yet the ability to interview well has a direct impact on whether you land the job you want.**

There are a couple of messages here. Number one: You're probably not an expert at interviewing. Number two: This process isn't something you want to be *too* comfortable with. Trust me. You don't ever want to be in and out of positions often enough that the job search feels natural.

Yet, if the ability to interview well has an undeniable impact on whether you get the job of your dreams (or even a job you think you'll like a lot), wouldn't you want to learn and maintain sharp interviewing skills? Of course!

MY GOAL IN WRITING THIS BOOK IS THREEFOLD.

FIRST, I want to tell you what's really going on in executive interviews. **SECOND**, I want to dispel myths that there are code words or preplanned answers that assure you interview success. **THIRD**, I want to share with you, simply and plainly, what *works*. I'll tell you what you need to do in your executive interviews to be at your absolute best. I'll let you in on the secrets to interviewing success.

Let me share a few more details of my expertise in executive interviews.

1. I get to see an amazing range of candidates up close. As part of my role as an executive recruiter, I've interviewed candidates for many different jobs, including CEO, chief financial officer, vice president of human resources, director of research, vice president of operations—and the list goes on. I've interviewed candidates for sectors such as manufacturing, higher education, nonprofit, financial services, consulting, and many others.

My goal in interviewing candidates is generally to determine the fit between the candidate and the job for which I am recruiting. As I discern that degree of fit, I consider the following:

- **SKILLS.** What specific abilities does the candidate bring—subject matter expertise, technical skills, leadership savvy, decision-making or problem-solving experience, or more?
- **REQUIREMENTS.** What degrees, licensures, certifications, or positions are desirable or essential to the role?
- **INTEREST.** How seriously is the candidate considering this opportunity?
- **CULTURE.** How easily will this individual step into what I know of the organization's culture?
- **STYLE.** How will this person mesh with the most important stakeholders, including boss, staff, and board?

I can usually determine job requirements and fit for skills fairly accurately. But to understand nuances of an organization's culture and style, I need to interview and interact with clients. So at the start of every search, I meet with numerous staff and stakeholders to get my best sense of organizational culture. Is it fast or slow? Collaborative or individualistic?

Results-oriented or process-focused? What makes the organization different from a similar one a few miles away?

2. I help client organizations plan their executive interview process. Each organization is unique and each executive hire unique, and, where possible, I help the organization plan its process. What should be discussed? Who should participate in the meetings? For a recent client, I drafted detailed "scenario questions" so the candidates could speak to some very real potential challenges in the role. For another, I designed an interview process that involved no fewer than seven stakeholder groups. Not every organization needs or wants a lot of assistance. Larger organizations usually come with a sophisticated human resources department. Public organizations may have established processes that can't be altered. In any case, I am involved as needed and always informed of the interview plan.

3. I participate in the interview process from start to finish. My firm coordinates and sets up meetings with the client and candidates. We confirm arrangements. We field questions from all sides. Without going so far as to coach candidates, we do our best to let them know what to expect to keep interviews surprise-free. I frequently come up with interview questions for my organizational clients—although, just as often, they write their own. At every turn, I work to make all parties to the interview as comfortable as possible.

4. I observe interviews. I'm in the room when my candidates interview. I'm not *part of* the interview. In fact, I carefully seat myself out of line of sight, often in a corner. If a client invites me to join in ("We have room at the conference table, Marcia. Sit here."), I politely decline. My job is to watch. This is my most valuable lens into the executive interview process, because I see the candidate in real time, and I hear questions and answers and "nonanswers." I detect tone and body language, warm and cool. I notice how some candidates struggle to develop rapport while others fall into easy conversation, as if they're getting together with old friends.

5. I believe in the interview process. Good interviews lead to good hires. When the process brings out a candidate's credentials and style, I have the privilege of seeing organizations add best-fit talent to their teams. That great talent is what it takes to build and sustain great companies and nonprofit groups. And when candidates land best-fit jobs that maximize their backgrounds and personalities, they find fulfillment and opportunity. Everybody wins. In other words, when a hire is right, it's good for the universe.

> **I dedicate my career to helping individual candidates and client organizations find their best paths forward by getting relevant information out in the open for everyone's thoughtful consideration. I make that same promise to you.**

There aren't many raging new developments in interview techniques. But there are some, and my colleagues and I stay up on changes and best practices. As our clients do, we try new approaches to get to know candidates. We experiment with fresh questions and interview activities.

6. I see what wins jobs and what loses them. In all the executive candidate interviews I observe with prospective employers, I constantly see patterns and themes. I note common behaviors that result in candidates being moved forward. I also see what causes others to be thanked but not considered further. In other words, I know what works as well as what doesn't.

By the end of this book, you'll know what I've learned from my unique observation point at the back of the interview room. My hope is that this education will help you win your interview, land your next job, and find success and satisfaction along the way.

CHAPTER 3

WHAT BRINGS YOU HERE?

EMPLOYEES EXIST ON A CONTINUUM OF ATTITUDES TOWARD THEIR JOBS, living somewhere between "I love it" and "I hate it." Or "I can't imagine ever leaving" and "I'll take the first ticket out." People looking for new opportunities are either **propelled** by circumstances inside their organizations or **pulled** by what they hope is a more attractive situation outside them.

So what brings you to this book? Why are you interested in the topic of interviewing? Most importantly, what motivates you to gain the practical insights you need to win your own interview?

As an executive recruiter, I find two factors typically propel a person to explore outside opportunities.

One is **structural**. "The company is moving headquarters next year." "The organization has weathered four downsizings and restructurings." "The future here looks bleak."

The other factor that propels someone to look outside is **personal.** "I don't see eye-to-eye with my boss." "I've worked here for years, and I have no allies." "We merged departments, and I get no respect."

Any of these situations can have obviously high stakes.

If you're considering moving on because a friend swears to have a job that's more fun than yours, the choice to search is less dire but often no less powerful. You're pulled by the tantalizing possibility of a **better opportunity.** Maybe it's greater responsibility or bigger size and scope. Perhaps improved logistics, something closer to home. It might be a job title you're seeking. A situation with better work-life balance.

I do find that a few people enter the job market because of thoughtful career planning. You're way ahead of the curve if you wake up one morning and think, *I've got five years here and I'm short on skills X, Y, and Z. If I can land a job as an associate VP elsewhere, I'll shore up those skills and set myself up for even bigger things.*

You might be surprised that as a recruiter, I find that hardly anyone is looking for a different gig when I call. So I dig in without being pushy. "Where do things stand for you right now?" "Are you actively looking? Are you dabbling, checking around occasionally?" "Are you absolutely not looking—or can I interest you in a unique position?" "Where do you fall between 'locked in' and 'looking for the nearest exit'?"

Whether or not a candidate responds directly, I can almost always pick up the answer from what he or she says—or doesn't say—or from the tone of the conversation.

CANDIDATE PERSPECTIVES

Even when presented with the same information about an open position, candidates approach the job opportunity with wildly varying interest levels and different points of readiness to make a change. Why does this matter? Because it profoundly impacts how they present to a potential new employer. **A candidate's perspective often is the determining factor for winning an interview.** Let me explain.

☐ PERSPECTIVE: CAUTIOUS

"I'm really happy where I am. I'm not at all sure I want this or any other new job."

As my colleagues and I recruit executives, the cautious candidate is the person we encounter most frequently. We typically contact a potential candidate out of the blue because we have reason to believe his or her background and experiences will be a good fit for an opportunity we're representing. We rarely know anything about the person's interest in changing jobs or whether the specific opportunity we're representing will be enticing.

These candidates are usually gracious, cordial, and wary. They ask tough questions. They seek counsel. They carefully evaluate their own impressions at each stage of the recruitment process, and if they continue in the process, they do so with careful consideration. They understand that an executive-level recruitment process is largely an exercise in discernment. They know they can withdraw from the recruitment process at any time, and they often do.

☐ PERSPECTIVE: CURIOUS

"I think I might want the job, but I'm not 100 percent certain. I need to make sure it's a good fit."

The curious candidate finds the open position appealing from the start. This person is already open to change if the right opportunity comes along. A willingness to at least consider other possibilities might be fueled by the desire for a new boss, new organizational structure, or new parent company.

We find that this candidate is happy enough in his or her current situation but intrigued that there might be an even better fit somewhere else. This person is full of meaningful questions aimed at determining whether the new opportunity truly represents the best next step.

☐ PERSPECTIVE: DESPERATE

"I want this job! I want any job!"

The desperate candidate wants a job, ***needs*** a job, perhaps any job within reach of landing. This person might be in job transition, having exited a previous employer as part of a layoff, a planned transition, or an unexpected firing. In some cases, the candidate has quit willingly. Whatever the circumstance, just about any potential job opportunity gets this candidate excited. Desperate candidates envision and sell themselves as the "perfect" fit for a job (or for whatever else might be next on my list!).

The longer it takes to land a job or even an interview, naturally, the more pressure candidates feel. If they've been in a job search longer than expected, they're likely weary from the rigors of the search. They start to doubt themselves. They may come to believe they haven't landed something because they're too old, they make too much money, or something or someone from their past is undermining their ability to get a job. At this point, they may lose focus on seeking roles where they could deliver the most value to a potential employer. They fall into a mindset that any job is a good job.

Cautious. Curious. Desperate. Which candidate perspective tends to perform better in the interviews? I can tell you that in almost every case, the candidate who is hired comes from the first or second category. Here's why. These candidates bring a healthy mix of interest and questions. The cautious and curious are typically more judicious and often approach the process with a take-it-or-leave it attitude. At first blush, that mindset sounds cavalier or even rude. But they often outshine candidates who initially want the job more.

The more desperate the candidate, the more likely counter-productive interview behaviors will emerge. Candidates who have reached a point of desperation, for example, tend to talk more than they listen. They oversell what they can do and default to claims of "I will (or can) do anything." They often show up anxious and edgy, almost hyperfocused, in the interview. They often overprepare at the cost of authenticity. And because they've lost focus on what they truly do best, they're unable to objectively evaluate the job for what it is and what it isn't.

Sometimes candidates with desperate mindsets see recruiters and HR as roadblocks to getting their message through to a hiring manager, or to getting a job at all—unnecessary impediments to the process rather than valuable partners who help facilitate a good fit. These candidates, disproportionately, don't land the jobs. Yet they easily could.

My role as a recruiter positions me as a neutral resource playing go-between for my client firms and the candidates I present. At times, though, I catch myself inwardly rooting for a candidate who really, really wants the job. It's usually a candidate in transition.

Let's face it. A fair number of people picking up a book on interviewing are already in career transition. By chance or by choice, they're between jobs. Maybe that's you. If so, I need you to hear what I'm about to say.

I never mean to diminish the pain of being without a job. Losing a job can be one of the most traumatic occurrences in a lifetime. I know. I've been there myself. I admire the courage required to jump back into the job market, especially if you find yourself looking for work for the first time in many years.

At the same time, I want you to be aware that whenever you move into job-search mode with a lot at stake, you enter a danger zone. Desperation can arise for a lot of reasons, but it's extremely common among people in transition. It can be such a serious hindrance that many search firms won't present people in transition as candidates. I hate saying that. I've never been that way, and that's not my firm's practice. But there are search firms who, as a matter of policy, won't even consider a candidate in transition—regardless of the individual's résumé.

It's heartbreaking to watch candidates self-destruct in interviews. As a search consultant given the job of presenting the very best candidates to a client organization, I've found that desperate candidates often struggle in the interviews. This can embarrass our firm and frustrate the client interviewers. I hear feedback such as: "Why did you send that person to us? They talked the whole time." "They didn't listen." "They were agitated, aggressive, overly persuasive." "They didn't know when to stop."

The person who has less at stake in an interview almost always comes across as more thoughtful. Moreover, almost all executive roles require—and all interviewers seek—an unflappable confidence. But that self-assurance is tough to fake in an interview for those who don't feel it. Most of us aren't trained actors, and if we're feeling vulnerable, frightened, or at high risk for our family, we're rarely able to cover it up. That's approximately 99 percent of us.

What do you do with all of this? One fact is true: You can't bring it to the interview.

If you feel anxious or emotional, or you find yourself in a position of high risk, find other outlets to work through that. A phone screen isn't the place to process your personal journey. A face-to-face interview isn't the occasion to let your concerns or self-doubts leak out. Yet keeping everything bottled up inside rarely works. So where can you go to talk? Who among your colleagues or friends will listen? Is your spouse/partner supportive? Where can you access roundtables or professional associations? Should you hire a coach or see a therapist?

If you find yourself drifting into a desperate state of mind, I want you to know I empathize completely. As we move forward together in this book, I especially want you to hear the thoughts I share so you can show up at interviews presenting your very best self.

➜ ARE YOU READY TO INTERVIEW?

☐ **WHEN ARE YOU *NOT* READY TO INTERVIEW?** If you choke up discussing a prior position, you're better off declining an interview to do some more processing. If a question about a past employer triggers an angry response, get coaching or counseling before moving forward. If your sense of depression about being laid off or a feeling about a former boss is still *raw*, take time for introspection, coaching, and even therapy before beginning. If you can't share your background without feeling beaten down, pausing from your search for some practice can boost your confidence as you discuss your attributes.

Do you think these things don't happen in interviews? Trust me, they do. I've seen it all. I've seen candidates cry, pace the room, and pound the table. I've heard them yell at interviewers and interrupt every single question. I've witnessed them intimidate and accuse people at the hiring organization. One candidate I interviewed became so unhinged that *I* felt compelled to run out of the room.

☐ **WHEN ARE YOU READY TO BEGIN INTERVIEWING?** You're ready to interview when you possess solid self-awareness, openness to give-and-take discussion, and an overall positive style. You're ready when you're grateful, future-focused, and self-controlled. Interviews require you to put all your experience and skills on the table for others to probe, question, and evaluate. Interviews raise career events (being fired, laid off, downsized) that can be tough to talk about. They require self-disclosure at a depth we rarely go to with strangers.

An interview is a high-stakes event. Almost always, it's a one-shot event. If you blow a discussion with a potential employer, there's virtually never a do-over. You need to be primed to interview the moment an invitation comes, meaning the hard work needs to be done beforehand.

Do you still have work to do to be ready? Take time to undertake that crucial processing of your past experiences. When you've put the issues behind you, celebrate! Interviews await you, and, with them, a chance to consider what your future can bring.

CHAPTER 4

HIGH-STAKES INTERVIEWING

(how you see it—and how hiring organizations see it)

High stakes (from your perspective)

Anyone who steps forward to say, "Yes, I want to interview!" has chosen to enter a highly-charged process. After all, the steps (and missteps!) you take on your career path are life-altering. This is your livelihood—how you provide for yourself and your loved ones. It's your lifework and the meaning you attach to that—your definition of yourself and the notches you put in your belt as you advance in your career. This is your community—the network of relationships that make life fulfilling. All of this is on the line. The outcome of an interview will determine how you spend a large part of your waking hours for the next span of your life.

The process of interviewing opens up all the possibilities in the world, but there are also pitfalls. Here's what happens when you walk into an interview setting:

- You bring great credentials, yet you might flounder at simply being yourself.
- You have tremendous skills, yet you face the risk of rejection (you're one of who-knows-how-many applicants, and if there are five finalists, you face an 80 percent chance you won't succeed).
- You expose the deepest part who you are (what job seeker hasn't wondered, *Am I good enough?*).
- You risk all kinds of things going wrong—and sometimes it's true that what *can* go wrong *will* go wrong.

If you're going into an interview, you're at a pivotal moment. At the end of the day, the choice is yours whether or not to take this job.

The high stakes of interviewing can include making a tough decision to move from one organization to another. If you're currently employed, the choice is still rife with risk. You potentially disappoint your staff by leaving them. You might upset your employer by abandoning half-done projects. You are ending a chapter in your career, and you might feel angst over leaving a record of success. *I'm petrified because I have a great staff. I've groomed three people. We're doing great work. We've just won division of the year. Here I sit, and I can't even describe to you how frightened I'd be to leave.* Those are heavy issues.

You can be a thoroughly competent and confident person and acutely sense these thoughts and feelings swirling inside. Or you might be so competent and confident that you don't adequately prepare or focus. You've had great interview experiences before—why would this be any different?

Let's assume you're eyeing this high-stakes situation and feeling at least some amount of stress. I don't coach candidates I present because I want them to appear as they really are. But if someone asks for help, I'll say, "Jason, as you and I discussed, you came off a little too persuasive. It might be better to ratchet back a bit. You need to step back when you meet the client." As a candidate moves from meeting with me to interviewing with a hiring firm, the stakes only get higher.

I once rode in an elevator with a candidate interviewing for a VP position at a company famed for its understated elegance. I had 500 feet of upward elevation to say to the candidate, "I know you're feeling the pressure. But we need to pull back a bit on the persuasion and forward behavior." Five minutes later we're in the interview. What I said was obviously still back in the elevator. He was verbose. Lengthy answers. Overselling.

Interviewers always start with some sort of a context-setting question: "Tell me about yourself." "Give me a little overview." "Why are you interested?" "Why do you think this is for you?" One woman I presented as a CFO candidate nervously attempted to squeeze 20 answers into that one question because she just couldn't risk not getting around to talking about every skill and background fact. She was the best candidate on the slate. Because she was anxious and talked too much, however, the organization took a pass on her and hired someone who (in my opinion) was a lesser candidate.

Here's what happens when someone goes on and on. Interviewers don't know how to take in far-flung answers that are all over the place. They get anxious because they know the interview is running overtime. Interviewers start scrambling and think about which interview questions they will have to forego asking because they have another commitment—perhaps another interview—after the scheduled time for this current interview. That uneasy feeling makes the candidate an outlier in a way that interviewers sometimes can't even explain. They'll say, "I just can't figure out Eric. I can't explain it, but he wouldn't be a fit." Well, it's because Eric missed out on answering half the questions. The committee wasted its time trying to figure out why he was all over the place.

Eric didn't mean to be disrespectful, but he messed with the process. And he lost the interview because of it.

High stakes (from an employer's perspective)

You might assume that interviewing is all about you. It's not. It's about what an organization needs and wants. And it's about the unique process it undertakes to determine the right hire.

There's a CEO, Board Chair, or other top leader behind ever executive hire. In a bit I'll introduce you to Deonne, the CEO in Petra's story of being hired as the vice president of sales and marketing position at Byhram Nash. **Consider the situation from a hiring executive's perspective.**

REALITY 1: THE HIRING EXECUTIVE IS USUALLY A VERY BUSY PERSON. You're probably a hiring executive yourself, so you know this to be true. You can expect the hiring boss to be highly scheduled to manage almost countless issues. He or she oversees an executive team and maybe hundreds or thousands or more employees, manages key relationships, and collaborates with the board. This person is not likely to interview unqualified candidates for the fun of it.

You can bet that the head of HR and the HR team will do everything possible in a recruitment process to ensure that only highly qualified candidates make it to the CEO's office. That isn't to say that a CEO can't take a flyer and meet a candidate who is a friend of a friend or from the CEO's alma mater, but that isn't typical. The trick is always bringing in qualified people small enough in number to be manageable but large enough to offer real choice. That pool sometimes expands out of fear that the right person might be unintentionally excluded. It's obvious that organizations use the interview process to see the best-qualified people, and that by seeing the right people, the odds of meeting and hiring the right person increase.

The pressure felt by hiring executives is actually good news for you. Ask yourself, "Would a busy CEO take an hour and a half to meet with me if not at least somewhat confident I can do this job? Would an HR executive or a search firm put his or her reputation at stake by putting me forward if not reasonably confident I'm a fit for this job?" You know the answer. Keep it in mind as you hear everything else I share.

REALITY 2: THIS HIRE MUST BE DONE RIGHT. Any executive position is critical to the organization's success, and the importance of an open role means that acquiring the right person matters to the organization, the CEO, the board, and other key stakeholders. This recruitment effort entails an extended process rather than a snap judgment, and a decision at its conclusion will be taken seriously!

Almost always, an executive hire creates both urgency and anxiety. Who will the person be? How will that person lead and manage people and fit our culture? Will she fulfill the hopes we have for this assignment? Does he have promotability potential for higher roles in the organization? These hires aren't taken lightly. They're often among an organization's most pressing issues.

As a business professional interviewing for a high-level job, think of the impact you'll no doubt have. You might have direct responsibility for hundreds of people working in your area. You may control millions of dollars in equipment. Perhaps you'll oversee the engineering of the company's next-generation products. Whatever your role, it's important. The stakes are high.

REALITY 3: INTERVIEWS ARE AN ORGANIZATION'S WAY OF MAKING A VERY EXPENSIVE DECISION—potentially the decision to hire you.

How expensive? Well, add up your prospective annual salary, include bonuses or other perks typical for your role, throw in 30 to 50 percent more for your employer-paid benefits package. Factor in the cost of travel you'll do, equipment you'll need, a portion of the cost of a supervisor you'll report to. There's probably more, but this will do. Multiply this figure times the number of years you expect to work in this job. *That's* how expensive a decision you are for an organization! Don't be surprised if the cost of the decision runs into the high hundreds of thousands of dollars.

Does this sound like a situation where a hiring organization is likely to be careless? Does it sound like "just anyone" will do?

Not only does an organization want to make a good decision; it wants to avoid a bad decision. A bad decision means a new hire doesn't work out for whatever reason. The costs from a bad hire include termination costs, the lost value of any onboarding or other training, the sinking morale of staff again pitching in to cover for a missing team member, disappointed clients weary of turnover, and lost time reopening the recruitment. The cost of a poor hire, just from an HR perspective, can easily equal a year's pay or even more.

All of this adds up without beginning to consider the millions of dollars in net gains or losses that could result from a new hire's leadership—or lack of it.

REALITY 4: AND THEN THERE ARE SKELETONS A HIRING ORGANIZATIONS IS UNLIKELY TO PUT ON THE TABLE. Maybe people in a department feel like they're dying. Sales are tanking in the southern region. They're down two staff members because those people followed another employee to a new organization. If they bring in a new hire and it doesn't work out, the whole company is at risk. They've been working on

ISO 9000 certification for five years, and if the new hire can't help shore it up, they've lost a ton of work and money.

Later in the book we'll get at questions you can ask to elicit what you need to know to make an informed decision. Interviews are funny things in that way. We all have questions. We're all trying to assess. But no one plays all cards at once.

Often, the only way you uncover hidden issues is by making the most of your network. If you're interviewing at an organization where a friend is connected, that friend can tell you the real high-stakes stuff, like a program that's close to tanking.

For now, your takeaway is twofold. On one hand, a hiring executive's time is at a premium. On the other hand, an organization must be cautious to bring in the right person. The upshot is often a lengthy, arduous, or even invasive process. Organizations often have far more on the line as they make hiring decisions than we can ever know.

CHAPTER 5

THE SECRET TO WINNING YOUR INTERVIEW

When it comes to hiring senior talent, companies choose from an array of almost limitless hiring activities. They write job descriptions, position profiles, and competency reports. All the parties involved (certainly an internal human resources department and possibly as external search firm or consulting professionals) settle on a reasonable set of skills needed to excel in a role. Some hiring activities open a funnel of candidates; others screen them. Subsequent activities validate and check credentials. Many discerning eyes pore over résumés. Much hand-wringing happens before any candidate is called for an interview with the hiring executive.

Now here's where many candidates need a shift in mindset. Picture yourself getting an initial phone interview or an in-depth face-to-face meeting. When you're asked about your experience (and you will be), ***how*** you answer is more telling than ***what*** you answer. Why? I hinted at this a few pages back. If you're invited to interview with the hiring organization, it's highly likely that a conclusion has already been reached: You *can* do the job. **The interview exists to validate that conclusion and to select the candidate who will be the best fit.**

Monday Morning Staff Meeting

What I mean is this: **The hiring executive's goal is to envision the potential success or failure of each candidate on the job.** That includes picturing the candidate not only performing the basic duties of the job but also *being in* the job.

Hence, what I call the Monday Morning Staff Meeting analogy. By the time candidates meet with the hiring executive, they're probably seen as capable of performing whatever responsibilities come with the job. Sure, the interview will include lots of questions about *the job*. But the hiring executive is simultaneously evaluating a broader *fit*. **Given a pool of well-qualified applicants, the winner (and losers) in the quest to fill a role is determined on the basis of fit.**

There are many components to fit:

- Fit within the broader organizational culture
- Fit among a team of colleagues and peers
- Fit with the team that the person being hired will lead
- Fit with the CEO

All of the many "fit factors" to be considered come together as the hiring executive thinks about each candidate in the work environment—interacting with other leaders, sharing information, making key decisions. Indeed, the hiring executive is considering how the candidate will *be* as a member of the team. In other words, how will the candidate fare in the Monday Morning Staff Meeting?

Think about the most successful groups you've worked in. Recall times your boss convened the group for sharing information and strategizing, or perhaps discussion and decision-making. Whatever these gatherings were called, no matter which day of the week they convened, discussion happened and decisions resulted. In my own case, for most of my work life, whether working for others or as a partner at a regional search firm and a cofounder at Ballinger|Leafblad, there has been an organized convening of staff. Usually, it took place on Monday. Therefore, my brain naturally goes to an analogy of the Monday Morning Staff Meeting.

That Monday Morning Staff Meeting could happen on a Tuesday, Wednesday, or even Saturday, if you work weekends. It might wear the label of "staff meeting," "executive team meeting," or "leadership group meeting." What I'm really referring to are meetings and interactions where a position can really shine, where a CEO or hiring executive most needs the right fit to ensure organizational success.

I'm suggesting that in an interview, the most crucial task of the CEO (or the hiring entity) is to visualize each candidate in the job—discussing the work, participating on the team, and helping make decisions that impact the whole organization. In other words, the CEO is thinking about how the candidate will fit in and perform at the Monday Morning Staff Meeting.

HERE'S WHY THIS MATTERS TO YOU, THE CANDIDATE.

It's more important than anything else I can tell you. I see the most successful candidates behaving how executives would ideally act in a Monday Morning Staff Meeting. The least successful candidates display behaviors in interviews unwanted at the Monday Morning Staff Meeting.

What are these desirable behaviors? When people come to these all-important gatherings, how are they expected to behave? What does "the boss" really want?

To illustrate, let's envision a hypothetical work situation. There's a high-performing team of executives assembled at a staff meeting. These executives need to make an important decision by the conclusion of the meeting (aren't most of our business decisions important?). How do these high-performing individuals behave? I've asked many leaders this question and heard an astonishingly consistent set of answers:

- Most often, leaders mentioned these individuals are **honest**, meaning they tell the truth. You can trust they're forthright in what they share. They don't hold back or withhold material meaningful to the discussion.
- They're **authentic**. They're real. They don't play games. In a high-performing group, members don't play politics or push hidden agendas. They say what they mean and mean what they say.
- They're also **self-aware**. All members are comfortable with who they are (not only strengths but limitations) and can readily ask for feedback from others.
- They're **discerning**. In other words, they exhibit sound judgment, collecting useful information and applying it to make good decisions valued by others. These thoughtful people ***get it*** in a way that makes others glad the member is on the team.
- They're **results-oriented.** They know what needs to be accomplished, and they meet desired expectation. They're not easily lured offtrack. They understand the purpose at hand and do their part to bring success.

I call these qualities "universal attributes" because they're what every company everywhere looks for in their leaders. They encompass more than skill sets or credentials. They get at a candidate's core character.

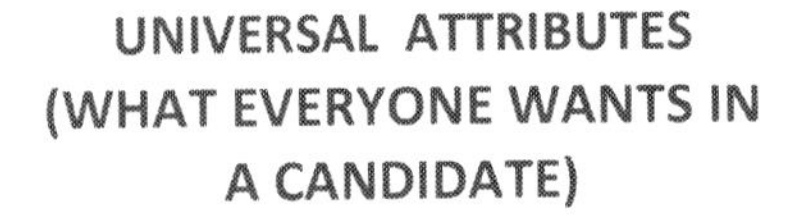

UNIVERSAL ATTRIBUTES (WHAT EVERYONE WANTS IN A CANDIDATE)

Honest

Authentic

Self-aware

Discerning

Results-oriented

So imagine again a high-performing work team at its Monday Morning Staff Meeting. This is an A-plus staff that makes the job of the CEO much easier. When they get together, it works. When they work in their own areas of expertise, they're trusted by the CEO. With this type of team, the CEO sleeps well. What characteristics do you think the CEO will look for in a new executive hire? What does the CEO need to see in you? These attributes!

The Monday Morning Staff Meeting analogy underscores the importance of universal attributes in an interview setting. It reminds you that while specific credentials are critical, these attributes trump credentials every time. Remember: If you've been asked to interview with an organization's top leaders, it's a fair bet that you possess all or most of the quantifiable job requirements.

Most of us understand these critical universal attributes. We all probably endeavor to develop them further. However, exhibiting them in an interview setting is far different. And far more difficult.

Once you are invited to interview, the hiring organization's evaluation of you moves from matching job requirements to seeing how well you articulate the connection between your experience and the new organization—**and most importantly, how well you fit.** Not just how you mesh with its mission or its ability to envision you at the Monday Morning Staff Meeting but, at a basic human level, **how well the organization likes you.** As you take part in conversations throughout the interview process, are you engaging, compelling, likeable?

This all might seem soft. Even fluffy. It's not. And, unfortunately, candidates often discount it while preparing for interviews. But how many times have you, as a hiring manager, selected the candidate you liked best? Have you ever selected the candidate you liked least?

What's really going on during an executive interview? The secret is this: When you're invited to meet with a hiring executive, your objective isn't to rigorously persuade that you're capable of doing the job. The interviewer is almost surely reasonably comfortable you can perform the job. You are, after all, among a select few whose background appears good enough to merit an invitation. **Rather, your objective is to be yourself and use your best powers of discernment to help the hiring executive decide—and to decide for yourself—if this is the right job for you and for the hiring organization. Period.**

Once you have that big fact in mind, I can tell you the best ways to prepare for and present yourself in your executive interview.

In part two of this book, I will walk you through the executive hiring process, framed in a point-by-point story, offering behind-the-scenes details at a hiring organization. I'll put you on the phone with organizational leaders and in the room with interviewers.

What's my point? On one level, the story is an ordinary tale, the stuff of everyday life in the world of organizations. But I have something more in mind. As I walk through crucial turning points, I'll draw on my experience to illustrate and explain what a hiring organization wants from you each step of the way—so that in the end you understand how to advance at each point of the interview process.

The interview process begins and ends with the critical truth that any job is about what an organization wants—not simply what *you're* looking for in your next position. That simple truth makes it essential for you to get into the mindset of the organization.

PART 2

INTERVIEWING FROM START TO FINISH

APPLICANT = someone who applies for a job

CANDIDATE = someone who meets the job's minimum qualifications (These people get tracked during the hiring process for affirmative action and EEOC requirements.)

CANDIDATE POOL = a pool of prequalified candidates

FINALIST = a candidate being considered for the job after going through a series of interviews

EMPLOYEE = the person who accepts the job offer

[CHAPTER 6]

BEHIND THE SCENES

(determining the need)

ON THE CEO'S MIND

Deonne Bratt Pennington was having a hard time feeling enthusiastic. At a Women CEOs meeting last week, the speaker called "filling a key organizational role" one of a leader's "greatest opportunities." Yet, as Deonne reflected on the current vacancy at Byhram Nash for a vice president of sales and marketing, she was definitely ***not*** envisioning the situation as a chance to unleash fresh growth. More on her mind were concerns about the role expressed by several executives, along with pressure to hire as quickly as possible.

As Deonne revisited the speaker's handout, one point caught her attention—the necessity for a hiring executive to really get to know what's needed in an open position.

Deonne grabbed her tablet and tapped in ideas to "really get to know" top needs:

- ☐ Meet with sales managers and marketing managers. (Together or separately?)
- ☐ Talk to VPs of manufacturing and engineering. (What are they looking for from sales and marketing? How could the partnership between functions be optimized?)

- [ ] Meet with select customers. (Get their thoughts on our sales and marketing group. Where are we strong? What could improve?)

- [ ] Read trade publications on trends in our sector. (What am I not seeing over the horizon?)

Deonne realized that gathering this information would take time, but with some concrete steps in front of her, she was beginning to sense this homework would be incredibly valuable. Then she added one more item to the list:

- [ ] Based on above, revise job description.

That task she could work on with her vice president of HR, Murray Wallace. Deonne glanced back over the list. *Hmmm, this could be a good opportunity for us after all.*

INSIDE HR

Murray Wallace looked at his watch. Five o' clock already? He wondered where the day had gone as he glanced down at his desk and his handwritten to-do list. ***Sure, a to-do list is a bit old-fashioned***, he thought, ***but it works. Usually.*** Murray liked the morning ritual of writing tasks for the day, carrying over undone activities from the day before and adding any new items that need to be accomplished. And (it always happens) more gets added to the list as each day goes on.

Recently named the vice president of human resources at Byhram Nash, Murray still felt pride in his new role. After 10 years in the company, in administrative jobs, as safety manager, and most recently as human resources director, Murray felt he was finally in a job that fit him perfectly.

With a great boss, terrific staff, and the chance to make a difference for 2,500 Byhram Nash team members throughout the region, Murray couldn t help but shake his head in awe and feel grateful for his good fortune. The last few months had definitely been the best in his career. Even his son had noticed his upbeat demeanor. "Daddy, you've been happy a lot," Orrie had said from the back seat the other day. "Are you getting a new car?" Murray smiled at the recollection.

But Murray's reverie was short-lived. The buzz of his phone startled him. It was Deonne. Murray picked up and grabbed a pen. "Hey, Boss!"

"Hi, Murray." Deonne Bratt Pennington's voice was clear and crisp. She had started her career in radio and still projected a powerful sound. When Murray attended his first all-employee meeting at Byhram Nash, he noticed right away how easily she commanded a group's attention. "Where are we on the recruitment for the new vice president of sales and marketing?"

Murray hesitated, but only for a second. He was managing this project closely, and he was prepared. The recruitment of this senior executive position was a critical project, highly visible for Murray, and he recognized an early opportunity to make a positive impression on his boss.

Confident, Murray replied. "Don't worry, Deonne, I haven't forgotten. I promised you a project update every Friday, and technically," he smiled as he spoke, "it's still Friday." He grabbed the project folder from his desk and flipped through its contents. "We're off to a good start."

Murray recounted the work that had gone into tweaking the job description for the vice president of sales and marketing position. "The bones of the document were still good," he remarked. "It just needed updating." Indeed, Joe Roth had been in the VP role for nearly nine years, and some of the job's specific responsibilities had changed.

As he had worked on tweaking the job description, Murray asked for input from key stakeholders to be sure the must-have skills and qualifications were included. The more he knew about the role, the more he could share with candidates. And, he knew the old adage "*The best candidates ask the toughest questions.*" Murray went on to describe to Deonne how the job had been posted on the company's internal job board as well as the external listings on their company website. "I know we don't think there is a likely successor in-house, Deonne, but I do value both the openness and potential referrals that come from internal postings." He flipped a page in his folder. "The thinking behind our open posting policy seems to work."

"That's great," Deonne agreed. "Thanks. Where are we with external recruiting?" Murray was ready for that question as well. "I've engaged Wynn & Zehring, a local executive search firm." He paused. "They've done several senior sales and marketing searches in our area, and I like their approach."

"I've heard of them," Deonne replied. "Aren't they the group that focuses on fitting the candidate to the client culture?"

Murray suddenly realized that he probably should have run this decision by Deonne. She didn't say so, but he filed the thought away for future reference. "*Fit first*—that's their motto," he answered. "Esther Joyce from Wynn & Zehring will work with me on this. Esther and I worked together years ago and I trust her. Our team is meeting with Wynn & Zehring next week, I've asked them to call you for input, and I've put several interview blocks for next month on your calendar as well.

"All good," replied Deonne. "You know we needed this person yesterday, right."

Murray knew the pressure Deonne and others were feeling. "We sure do. Thanks for the conversation," he finished. "You saved me from a long email report. I'm crossing it off my to-do list right now!"

CHAPTER 7

ARE YOU UP FOR THE JOURNEY?

JOB SEEKERS QUICKLY ENCOUNTER THE MADDENING REAL- ITY THAT EVERY ORGANIZATION HAS A DIFFERENT HIRING PROCESS. Some routes move directly to the goal, while others seem to meander. Some bring many insiders along on the journey; others, just a few key decision-makers. Some focus almost solely on interviews, yet others add psychological assessments, test batteries, presentations, and virtually limitless other options.

I can't say for a fact that there's a single most common way to hire, especially at an executive level. About the only thing that is (almost) absolutely certain is that you'll be interviewed, and in most cases, you'll be interviewed more than once.

That isn't news.

What goes unseen by candidates are scores of tasks happening within a hiring organizing. You've probably been there. Compared with the few hours a candidate gets to interact with a company, the amount of time and energy invested behind the scenes, from many players, is significant.

Organizations are running lean, with no room for extra staff. They're constantly reevaluating job descriptions, skill gaps, and most-needed qualifications. They ride trends of structures and reporting relationships. They press on through budgetary tightening and loosening. As they manage their key talent, organizations vary in their ability to define their needs, and priorities may change as they begin the process of hiring. Some organizations generate a long list of qualifications for a candidate that might not exist in the real world; others focus on a few core competencies; and what anyone is looking for may evolve when meeting actual candidates. In the context of all these moving parts, a hiring team does its best to gather meaningful information about a potential candidate to inform its decision:

FROM A RÉSUMÉ:

- What skills does the person possess?
- What is this persons background?
- What similar work has she done?
- How long is he likely to stay with us?

FROM WRITTEN COMMUNICATIONS:

- How well does this person express herself in writing?

FROM JOB REFERENCES:

- What do others say about him?
- Where has she been most successful?
- How has he gotten along with people in other jobs?

AND FROM INTERVIEWS:

- How can she apply her skills to this unique job?
- How can he translate his experience to our broader organization?
- How will this person fit our culture?
- How will she get along with people here?
- How will he represent our organization?
- How much do we like her? Do we want to work with her?

By the time an organization invites you to interview, you can be sure your résumé has been reviewed and your experience vetted. The goal of interview conversations, therefore, is to bring out nuances of background and applied skills. Most importantly, the interview team will aim to uncover your fit in terms of team, culture, personality, and more.

Just as a hiring team does its homework, you need to do yours. I've said there are three types of candidates—the cautious, the curious, and the desperate. We all exist on a continuum of interest from ambivalence to extreme enthusiasm. As an organization indicates interest in you, it's time for you to grapple with your interest in the organization and to voice that appropriately throughout the process.

EXPRESSING INTEREST

First things first. The start of an interview process is prime time for you to begin to gauge and communicate your interest. You don't have time to waste on a far-fetched possibility, nor does a hiring organization. While some candidates accept interview opportunities "for practice," I have no stomach for that at the executive level. Taking jobs for a spin can breed a reputation that organizations won't take seriously. Whatever your interest, or lack thereof, speak and act with authenticity.

Suppose you own your own company, and your team is blowing the roof off. Or every aspect of your current employee role pleases you. Or you're nearer to retirement than anyone suspects. Any of these situations and many more could put you in a somewhat rare category of people who'd never consider leaving a current role for another. These people exist. I've been on the phone with them. If you find yourself at the "I would never consider a different job" end of the continuum, that's okay. If an opportunity is presented to you, a simple "No thanks, I'm not open to a new position at this time" works just fine.

Perhaps you want to qualify that response. You might be open to other opportunities even though you're closed to *this particular job.* Maybe a competitor is hiring and there's rancor between organizations. Or you know for a fact that you dislike the work, culture, or management of the hiring organization. If your reaction to *this* possibility is "No way!" but you might say "Why not?" to another, be clear about your intentions.

If you sense at all that you would consider a position, proceed carefully. Don't pretend a higher interest than you have. Say, "I might be interested in something like this, but I need to be honest. I have a number of questions."

What do you *need to know*?

Do you have a handle on what you *don't yet know*?

There are plenty of situations where you lack all of the information you need to get a feel for whether this is a good or bad fit. Honestly, you're torn. Your current job has positives, and you can see potential upsides in the new role. When you're just not sure where a possibility will go, you might feel you should bottle up that inner debate. Sharing with the hiring organization what you see as the pluses and minuses of an opportunity isn't a bad move, however, especially if it lets the company address your concerns.

Of course, you may have good reasons for enthusiasm. Suppose you have inside knowledge of the organization and job. You've done your homework, and what you've learned is excellent. You feel thoroughly encouraged, even with a few remaining items that need checking out. It's more than okay to say, "I'm excited about this position. I have some questions I need to address, but I'd like to continue the dialogue."

At the far end of the excitement continuum is the feeling that a job is ideal, where everything checks out to your liking. Wow! It's your dream job.

The faster and further you move toward flat-out excitement about a position, the more I want to pull back on the reins. In fact, I outright urge you to slow down, especially when you're near the start of an interview process.

Enthusiasm is fantastic. Yet I'd argue that no job is perfect. Have you really asked *all* the questions necessary to clarify whether the position is right for you? Even as you express your keenness for the job, you're wise to prop the door open (just a bit) for issues that might arise. "Wow!" you could say. "This job seems like it's exactly what I'm looking for. I think I could really contribute. A question or two might come up, but I can't see anything getting in the way of my wanting to pursue the opportunity. I'm highly interested."

There's no good or bad place to be on the interest continuum. Just get clarity about where you are in the process. When you're on the "less interested" side of the continuum, ask tough questions! Trust your instincts that this opportunity might not be right for you at this time while remaining open to additional information that could change your mind. When you're on the "more interested" side, don't neglect your due diligence! The heady rush of being sought after by an organization can blind you to issues you should be addressing.

Remember, the interview process you're entering is twofold. The hiring organization moves along its own continuum. It needs to be convinced you're *the one*. Meanwhile, you're moving along the interest continuum. You need to be persuaded this job is *the one*. Be attuned to what you already know and what you still need to discover, and then let your experience of the process and the facts you learn along the way determine your interest.

CHAPTER 8

FIRST POINT OF CONTACT

ESTHER JOYCE FACED A TIGHT DEADLINE. AS A MEMBER OF THE WYNN & ZEHRING TEAM WORKING WITH MURRAY WALLACE, she was helping to recruit and manage the candidate pool for VP of sales and marketing at Byhram Nash. A couple of internal candidates expressed interest. A couple of folks arrived via applications on the search firm's website. Others became engaged in the process through referrals. And Wynn & Zehring recruited additional candidates. All told, there were twenty potentially viable candidates interested in exploring the position.

Esther was wishing she'd set aside more hours for the initial vetting. Oh well! Lesson learned for next time. Now the task was hers. **She discussed the prescreening criteria with Murray, and they agreed it made sense to have the firm do an initial assessment and vetting of candidates before a deeper review of final candidates.**

While Esther's firm was brought in to recruit a slate of candidates, it also moved the process along by undertaking several critical activities:

- Conducting research to identify potential qualified candidates by industry and function
- Reviewing applications

- Thoroughly evaluating résumés and CVs
- Checking LinkedIn pages and other online biographical information
- Performing telephone screening interviews
- Facilitating in-person interviews
- Checking references
- Coordinating assessments

Not every executive hire involves an external recruitment firm, but Esther knew that she and her firm would add significant value in this hiring process. Murray himself told her that he valued Wynn & Zehring's functional expertise as essential for a hire of this consequence. The search firm would know of people that Murray himself could not find. Moreover, Murray shared that his human resources team and other key players didn't have capacity to conduct an extensive search without the assistance of a third party.

CHAPTER 9

YOUR FIRST STEP

YOUR FIRST POINT OF CONTACT into a hiring organization can originate from many directions.

You may have initiated the interaction by submitting a résumé or applying for a job via the organization's website. In most organizations, it falls to the human resources department to follow up on job inquiries and applications. Your interest could trigger a response from an HR professional who might be very inexperienced (an intern) or very senior (an HR executive). Neither scenario is necessarily *bad*, although rarely is an intern the right person to query about details of an executive role or to get a take on the organization's managerial culture.

Savvy HR leaders increasingly attempt to recruit proactively. Aware that many quality candidates will never see the organization's job postings, they go hunting for talent. If you've applied for a job at an organization in the past, a forward-looking HR professional might have kept your materials (some actually do!) and might approach you to discuss a new opening. In any case, remember that anyone reaching out from human resources works for the hiring company. An HR person isn't a neutral party and is less likely to be forthcoming with feedback or insider details.

YOUR FIRST CONTACT could very well come from an external recruiter. You might already be looking for your next opportunity and welcome a recruiter's call or the contact might catch you by surprise.

Recruiters possess varying amounts of information about a particular job and company. Some bring up-close knowledge of the organization and the people hiring for the open position. Some know less, even to the point of never having met the hiring executive. A recruiter's level of knowledge is usually based on whether he or she is retained, contingent, or contract (more on those differences in a moment). Although external recruiters work for and represent the organizations that hire them, keep in mind that they may be more willing than internal recruiters to offer you professional guidance, interviewing pointers, and in-the-moment feedback.

YOUR INITIAL CONNECTION to a hiring organization may come via your network. Perhaps a friend or professional contact referred you. Maybe you already have a direct relationship with an employee of the hiring organization. If getting an interview results from your networking, someone might have already vouched for you and your fit for this position, putting in a good word for you. This offers your candidacy a tremendous jump start; don't take this advantage lightly. Have you reached back to thank your networking contact? How will you keep your contact updated on your progress throughout the interview process?

Regardless of the origin of your first point of contact or the rank or role of the person who reaches out, honor that contact for what it is: indication that an organization thinks you have great qualities and wishes to explore a career opportunity with you. **Treat that first contact with warmth, gratitude, and respect. Whenever a recruiter or potential employer calls, it's always a compliment!**

Working with recruiters

When you're at the executive level, there's a good chance a recruiter has reached out to you to initiate an interview process. Recruitment firms, sometimes also called executive search firms, are of two primary types: contingency and retained. There's also a third, less common type: contract.

Contingency firms are contracted by organizations to recruit candidates and send over résumés of qualified individuals. The client organization might hire a few or several such firms to source candidates for the same position. If a firm presents the successful candidate, it is paid a fee—that is, the firm has a contract for payment *on contingency*. A contingency recruiter knows that other firms and possibly the client organization itself might be recruiting some of the same people, and therefore might be cautious at first about revealing the identity of the hiring organization. This recruiter might refer to the hiring organization without naming it, as in "The company is an international chemical manufacturer" as opposed to "Our client is Warren+Robinson."

Contingency firms usually work on many open searches at a time. Because they want to be the first firm to present the successful candidate to the client, they often move very quickly.

Expect a contingency recruiter to review your résumé and interview you, perhaps via telephone, before presenting your résumé to the client organization. They will likely assist with setting up your interview but may not be heavily involved in debriefing the interview or in offer negotiation, if you get to that point.

Some contingency recruiters build histories with particular client organizations and can provide helpful insights about the staff, culture, and more. Others bring limited knowledge about the hiring organization and key players. As the interview process unfolds, be alert to that potential gap.

Retained firms are hired by the client organization to recruit candidates for a specific position until the role is filled. Retained search firms contracted *on retainer*, meaning they have an exclusive search role on each project and commit to continued recruitment until a successful candidate is selected. A retained recruiter usually works on only a few searches at a time and will tell you immediately which organization he or she represents. "Hello, Janese. I'm contacting you today on behalf of Community Organizing Partners."

Recruiters working on retained search usually have met with several members of the hiring organization, typically investing enough time up front to get to know the organization, staff, and culture very well.

As a result of all these factors, retained recruiters typically interview and vet candidates more thoroughly before presenting a slate to the client organization. In fact, you should expect a more thorough, perhaps even onerous, process if you participate in a retained search. Expect a phone screen with the recruiter as well as a lengthy in-person interview. You will likely be asked to complete a written assessment or questionnaire.

A primary difference between recruitment firms is their relationship and their contract with the hiring organization.

This can impact your experience as a candidate. Since contingency firms generally work on many searches at a time, their phone screen might be briefer than a retained recruiter's interview—10 minutes versus 40 minutes, for example. And a contingency recruiter may or may not meet you in person, instead moving you quickly to a client interview the next week, whereas you might wait a month before getting an interview in a retained process.

It's never wrong to ask a recruitment firm about its arrangement with the hiring organization. "Are you working on retainer?" isn't an offensive question.

Contingency recruiters may have done multiple placements at an organization, and this helps the recruiter know the place and its people well. Don't hesitate to ask Jim the recruiter if he has done other searches with the client organization, or how many people at the hiring organization he has met with.

By representing a company exclusively, retained recruiters often have tighter connections and may be privy to more confidential information. Retained firms are more likely entrusted with searches for higher levels of candidates.

Contract recruiters represent a third approach in the executive search world. They look for and place executives interested in time-limited assignments, such as at an organization that needs a VP of finance with expertise in turnaround efforts for a year or two, or at a nonprofit that wants an interim CEO for a few months as it regroups and redirects after the departure of a long-tenured founder.

I find that many senior executives who choose the contract path are looking for a way to contribute to one or two more organizations before scaling down in their career. Younger leaders might use a contract role to jump-start a consulting career composed of serial full-time positions or part-time engagements serving multiple clients, each needing just a portion of their time.

It's up to you whether you consider these positions. For some leaders, they are the perfect next step. Note that the same recruitment firms that seek to fill full-time, permanent executive positions may also conduct searches for contract candidates.

Regardless of the type of recruitment firm you're working with, view the recruiter as a potentially valuable resource as you prepare for your interview.

The recruiter might be coordinating the interview, and will assist with logistical details like scheduling and location. She or he should provide the address of the interview along with names and titles of people you will meet and the projected length of the interview.

In addition to essential details, the recruiter can likely provide *much more* information that could be helpful. Don't hesitate to reach out to the recruiter as you prepare. If you have several questions, ask to set up a specific time for discussion. Don't launch into a lengthy set of questions without asking if it's a good time to talk.

Here's a starter list of information you might request from a recruiter prior to an interview:

- Have you met the interviewers? How would you describe their personalities?
- Have you placed anyone with this client in the past? What feedback did you get from candidates you placed there?
- Do you have a sense of the types of questions they will ask me?
- Are there specific topics or questions I should prepare for?
- Are you aware of how they view my background (strengths and areas of concern)?
- Based on your interaction with these individuals, do you have any other tips or advice for me?

No matter how much you've researched the hiring organization, the recruiter probably has more—and more accurate—information than you do. Grab every opportunity to capture the recruiter's thoughts and benefit from his or her wisdom. While the recruiter might not have ready answers for every question, you should still ask.

After your interview, you should also ask the recruiter for feedback:

- What specific feedback did you get about my interview?
- What stood out as my strengths? Did any areas not show up as well?
- Did you get a sense of what they thought about my fit with their culture?

- What should I change stylistically in the next interview?
- How would you recommend I prepare for the next interview?
- Based on what you heard, what do you suggest I do differently next time?

Don't neglect the chance to get free counsel from someone who has worked closely with the hiring organization.

I'm personally surprised how often candidates *don't* ask me for my thoughts and impressions about the client organization and what I know about the upcoming interview. By the time I'm scheduling interviews, I've had many conversations with the hiring organization. I usually help in shaping the position description. I learn exactly which skills and characteristics matter most to them and why. I've experienced the personalities of the interviewers. When candidates ask me questions on any of these topics, I'm happy to share. At length, if desired. But if candidates don't ask, they don't learn.

I recently sat in on an interview for president of a large professional association. One candidate, Jerome, presented himself as a visionary leader with outstanding communication skills. Indeed, the panel was captivated by his humor and his ability to engage. He shared examples of how he connects successfully with members and staff alike. Based on my own interview with him, I felt he was an outstanding candidate.

Yet, after the meeting, the committee expressed concerns. They didn't sense Jerome had either passion or skill for the organization's programs. Although he had those abilities, Jerome glossed over them in the interview. His candidacy was forwarded to the next round of interviews, but just barely.

When I contacted Jerome, he asked for my feedback. I told him that parts of his background and skills (vision, strategy, and stakeholder communication) came through loud and clear. I added, however, that he had missed opportunities to explain his programmatic management background (and he had won national awards for program innovation!).

Jerome accepted the feedback and put it to work in the next round. I watched him tactfully weave in concrete examples of his program leadership. He mentioned some of the awards he'd won for program growth and innovation. When Jerome was offered the position of president, he readily accepted!

CHAPTER 10

NARROWING THE POOL

AS ESTHER JOYCE DELIBERATED HOW TO CONTINUE THE VET- TING OF CANDIDATES FOR VICE PRESIDENT OF SALES AND MARKETING, she did some quick mental math (number of calls multiplied by time allotted per person) and carved out three afternoons to conduct phone screens. These brief but revealing interviews would help her further narrow the pool. The task felt daunting: Wynn & Zehring had high standards for all parts of the process, phone screens included. Esther had looked through enough of the résumés to see many high-quality sales and marketing leaders. But Byhram Nash had requested a slate of approximately six candidates. *Six candidates?* she thought. *I'm not sure I can get to just six!*

Faced with her immediate task of calling candidates, she worried about running into a talker; if any of the candidate calls were to go significantly over the allotted time, she would be late for her one sane moment of the week, a yoga class that started at 6 p.m. sharp.

Esther dialed the first number. Her usual procedure was to ask six to eight questions to determine whether the applicant was qualified to advance into the candidate pool. She always found it interesting to meet new people by phone. Why were they considering a role at Byhram Nash? And what made them tick?

The first person had picked up right away. "Hello?" came

the answer. When Esther introduced herself, the candidate stumbled. "Who are you? Why are you calling me?" Not an auspicious beginning to the relationship. The candidate tried to remedy a poor start, but the first impression had been made. Now it was time for another candidate, another call, another person Esther would do her best to get a sense of. This candidate's voice sounded calm and self-assured. "This is Petra. May I help you?" Esther glanced at her notes and began the conversation.

In this phone screen, Esther sought only to ensure a basic fit for the job. Full-blown interviews would come later. The senior executive recruiter was also scheduled to conduct another set of calls for in-depth job and skill review.

Petra graciously followed Esther's lead, answering questions as Esther asked them. At the end of the call, Petra thanked her for her consideration and time. She asked about next steps of the process. Fair enough. Esther replied that either the senior executive recruiter from Wynn & Zehring or she herself would call candidates back with a status report within three days. The next step for a smaller group of selected candidates would be an interview with the CEO, Deonne Bratt Pennington. If Petra were to move forward, the interview would occur within the next couple of weeks, if possible.

Esther hung up. *Very capable person,* she thought. *Really easy to talk to.*

Several other candidate calls went equally well. *These candidates are great*, Esther thought. *Piece of cake!*

Esther had discovered that her initial contact trips up many people, forgetting that a first call is a first call. They come on strong, attempting to persuade their way into the job. She was always turned off by a heavy persuasion style. Or when a candidate peppered her with questions, pushing for details way beyond what even a well-prepared external consultant would know about a job at a client company. Picky questions definitely don't score points.

Not in this case, though. No, these were gracious candidates. Each had meaningful experience and seemed to get how to interact in an initial contact. Smooth calls. Done on time. Esther grabbed her briefcase, turned off the office light and headed to yoga.

CHAPTER 11

SURVIVING THE PHONE SCREEN

MANY INTERVIEW PROCESSES (MOST?) BEGIN WITH A PHONE CONTACT. SOMEONE—LIKELY A RECRUITING MANAGER OR HUMAN RESOURCES PROFESSIONAL—sets up a time to talk with you by phone. Usually nothing more than a half hour or so. Typically one-on-one rather than a conference call.

To attain the goal of determining whether to move your candidacy forward, the person on the other end of the phone needs to answer two basic questions. First, are you *feasible* as a hire? Second, are you possibly a *fit* for the organization?

The feasibility question ensures that nothing obvious would preclude you from taking the job if selected. Depending upon the position, you might get inquiries like these: "Can you relocate?" "How much can you travel?" "Are you able to attend weekend conferences?" "Our office is located an hour north of the city—does that location work for you?"

Other questions could include "What compensation range are you looking for?" (more on how to respond to that in the next chapter!) and "Our small organization doesn't offer health care benefits—is that acceptable for you?"

Or you might be asked, "You're currently a vice president—in this role are you okay with the title of director?" or

"We're working to fill this position quickly so the new general manager can be at our international conference about 45 days out—is that workable?"

These questions flush out candidates unable to accept an offer despite even the best fit. The questions are short and straightforward, as should be your answers. If you can't travel, say so. If the job requires daily office presence and the commute would kill you, thank the interviewer and decline further consideration. Don't lie or obfuscate reality in the hope that the hiring organization will miraculously change its mind about key factors. That rarely happens. Be scrupulously honest and let things unfold as they must.

The *fit* question determines whether a candidate *might* be right for the role and organization. It decides whether the organization will invite you in for a longer conversation to fully assess fit. My business partner equates this process of rapidly filtering candidates to speed dating. After a short discussion, only one question matters: *Do I want to see this person again?*

Every time you answer your phone for a screen, remember this crucial point: A phone screen isn't an interview. It's shorter. It usually involves talking with someone other than the hiring manager. Your goal, therefore, is *not* to wedge into this brief conversation every glowing fact of your career and accomplishments. Err on the side of answering briefly. Long stories or illustrations are usually best saved for an in-person audience. The interviewer likely has a few select questions about your background and might want detail on just an item or two from your résumé. Answer those questions without trying to fill in what you think the interviewer needs!

Here's the bottom line: Allow the interviewer to control the discussion.

Even during a quick phone screen, you might be asked if you have any questions. The topics on your mind at this point are likely fairly general, but carefully stick to questions appropriate to this early stage of an extended process. Assume you'll get time to ask two or three questions at most. And remember who you're talking with. If you're on a call with a company's HR professional, save your question about what the hiring manager has in store for next year's product launch.

These candidacy-killing mistakes happen far too frequently in phone screens:

- **Too much talking, not enough listening.** Candidates who use the phone screen to make their pitch and dominate the discussion rarely get invited to a face-to-face interview.
- **Too many questions, inappropriate questions for this early stage, or questions asked of the wrong person.** I'll just say it. Picky, prying, or deep-dive questions are generally not helpful at this stage.
- **Failure to do your homework about the job and organization.** I know if a candidate is prepared. Your tone should communicate that the job and organization interest you. It's alarming how often I conduct a phone screen and the candidate asks, "What job is this again?"

As you answer that call for a phone screen, have a positive, gracious style and presentation. Don't dominate. Say thank you. Don't forget the speed-dating analogy. Remember what's first on the screener's mind: *Do I want to see this person again?*

I was talking about interviewing with an executive I really wanted to help. When I brought up phone screens, he grew angry. "Oh, those screeners," he fumed. "They're just looking for reasons to rule you out. How am I supposed to get past those idiots? What do I have to do?"

I said a phrase that frequently pops into my mind. "Are you open to feedback?"

"Well, yeah."

"You know what?" I said. "Those people on the other end of a call are looking for a coworker." I paused to let that sink in. "They're thinking··· *Hey, here's a guy who's going to be few steps down the hall from me. I'm going to have to interact with him. And if he doesn't work out, people are going to blame me for letting him through*."

And then I had to be really honest. "You're looking at a role where you'll be a company leader," I continued, "and they can't picture that. My hunch is they don't like you very much because you feel disdain for them, and it's coming through loud and clear."

This stage of the interviewing process—okay, and other stages as well—might cause you to feel frustration toward recruiters, HR team members, administrative assistants, basically anyone in the process other than the decision-makers. Lots of candidates see all of us "others" as a necessary evil (a view I hear often). Even worse, others assume an attitude that we're blocking them from getting the job.

That's a mindset you can't cover up. I can promise you

that this attitude is not only incomplete but also erroneous in the extreme. It won't serve you well.

If you show up at interviews with prejudgments about the HR function, staff, recruiters, whoever, you do two incredibly harmful things.

First, your attitude causes you to miss an opportunity to learn. The people you see as roadblocks can throw open a window to an organization's culture and give you a wide-open view. They know the place and people up one side and down the other. They might offer their impression of the hiring manager. (Some might *do* an impression of the boss.) These folks can answer probing questions you're almost afraid to ask—things you might not be able to learn from anyone else in the process. They know where the organization's skeletons hang. What an opportunity!

Second, your attitude endangers your candidacy. Every person you meet throughout the interview process is a golden opportunity. If you think otherwise, those people will sniff you out. They will sense hostility, and they can easily shut you down. Why would they ever put you forward?

Interviewing can feel like a confusing, long-way-around process. But here's an attitude you want to take with you each step of the way: Whenever you struggle, ask yourself these questions, in your inner dialogue or even a journal: *What can I glean from this? What can I pick up about winning that role I really want? What can I discover about myself? What can I learn about fit? Isn't this all fascinating? I get to talk to someone else!*

Most people I call see me (a seasoned recruiter) as an ally. Do they all use me to full extent of what I can provide? Not often enough.

I had a CEO series of interviews where each candidate had to give a presentation. I worked with the hiring committee of the organization to design the presentation portion of the upcoming interviews. Then I needed to call the candidates to set up the interviews. I proactively set up calls with each candidate ahead of time, offering coaching on what to do. *Marcia Ballinger, former public-speaking coach, at your service. I'll help in any way I can. I know the search committee. I've sat with them for hours. I'll share any information I'm able to—**if only you ask**.* I told each aspiring CEO, "Please call me." Did even one person get back to me and say, "Here's what I'm thinking about for my presentation—how does that strike you? Here's my handout—could you take a look?" None did. Hmmm.

CHAPTER 12

HOW TO ANSWER THE MONEY QUESTION

AT SOME POINT IN THE PROCESS, SOMEONE WILL POP "THE MONEY QUESTION." THE QUESTION MIGHT SOUND LIKE "Tell us about your salary requirements" or "What are you thinking about, compensation-wise, for your next job?"

The questioner's goal is simple: Determine whether your salary expectations match the range for the job.

Asked early in the recruitment process, a money question helps the hiring organization decide if both sides are playing in the same compensation ballpark, or if a gap looms so large that talking further doesn't make sense.

The employer is not asking this question to be a jerk or to make you squirm. Bringing in a candidate for an interview can be extremely expensive, when you think about the hours required by all involved parties.

Again, this is a question. It's nowhere close to a job offer.

Note that I said "range." Virtually all professional jobs have a compensation range. The higher the level, typically, the broader the range. I've worked searches with a $100,000 compensation swing between the lowest- and highest-paid and both candidates were in the range.

If you work a similar job in a similar industry, your pay probably lands within range. If you work a similar job in a different industry but for a similar kind of company, you're probably in range. All things considered, you're likely in the ballpark.

The question about money or compensation is never just one question with a right or wrong answer. Compensation is far more complicated than that.

You're wise to mentally frame this money question not as that single item with a right or wrong answer but as an invitation to dialogue. Granted, if the position pays $75,000 and you want to maintain your current $150,000, the conversation might be over in a blink, but realize in advance that this topic is intended to be a discussion, not a quiz question.

> **What's so important about framing this question as the beginning of a conversation?** Because it takes the pressure off how you answer that opening question about money. Nevertheless, how you answer the first question sets up the dialogue that comes later, and so it remains very important.

To me, your best answer has three qualities: honest, self-aware, and brief.

- **Start any money discussion by being totally honest at all times.** If you're asked and are comfortable sharing your current pay, state it honestly. It isn't common, but I've known of employers who ask to see a document verifying salary. Before you begin looking at a new job, be prepared for this question. I mean that. You should know precisely how much money you make. If there are multiple components to your compensation (such as a base salary, management bonus, and participation in a long-term incentive program, for example), you should know the value of each component. If it makes sense for you, be ready to discuss these actual numbers.
- **You should also be self-aware.** You don't need to respond to the initial money question by divulging that you have

two children in college or unexpected bills to pay, but you do need to know your own situation. As the compensation discussion continues, be prepared to ask your own questions to obtain the information you need to decide if a role fits you money-wise. If your life situation requires that you score a significant raise at this time, you should know that compensation target. If your life situation allows space for a significant pay cut, know that too. I'm not suggesting that you lead with this information. Or even that you necessarily share it, if not required. You should just be in command of your own situation and accurately know your own financial requirements.

- **Your answer to the initial question about money should be brief.** Seriously. Resist the urge to offer up a lot of information or long salary history. When the money question comes up, answer it graciously. Concisely. Then sit back and wait for further discussion.

By the way, it isn't acceptable to play coy and avoid the money question. Consider the following possible answers:

THEIR QUESTION: "What is your current salary?"
UNACCEPTABLE ANSWER: "I don't know."

You do know. Or you should know. Even if you're paid through direct deposit and a significant other handles all the money, this answer sounds like you're really uninformed or are purposefully lying.

This does not mean that you must reveal your pay. Some states and jurisdictions have ruled it illegal for employers to request current compensation numbers from applicants, as this has been found to perpetuate lower pay rates for traditionally undercompensated groups, such as women and people of color. I believe that this trend will continue.

If you feel that you have been systematically undercompensated, you may wish to work from a discussion of your desired compensation range instead.

Remember that the money question is a dialogue. To take part in the dialogue, you need to be seen as honest and sincere.

THEIR QUESTION: "What are your salary requirements?"
UNACCEPTABLE ANSWER: "I believe you'll come up with a fair offer."

Um, that also sounds like you're not able or willing to participate in a dialogue about compensation. Remember, no one is drafting an offer at this point; they are seeing if pay expectations are in the ballpark, and if it makes sense to take the expensive step of having you come in to meet with several executives for the next interview.

Or

THEIR QUESTION: "What are your salary requirements?"
UNACCEPTABLE ANSWER: "I want your best offer. Whatever you think the job is worth."

This answer, again, doesn't open the door for dialogue. Remember that there isn't one magic number of what a job is worth. Pay will vary for someone with proven success versus someone new to the field who requires significant training. Many factors determine what any job is "worth," so don't avoid participating in the money conversation by trying to dodge it. You can't.

So how do you answer the money question? Your answer should address one of these questions: *How much do you currently make?* or *How much do you seek?*

Consider these examples:

THEIR QUESTION: "What compensation range are you seeking?"

YOUR ANSWER: "I currently earn $105,000 in base salary." (This doesn't include an upcoming cost-of-living adjustment, for example, or other perquisites.)

OPTIONAL ANSWER: "I currently earn $105,000 in base salary, although I have a cost-of-living increase of 3 percent coming next month."

OPTIONAL ANSWER: "I understand that the range for these jobs is around $105,000. I hope to be in that area."

What if you believe you're currently paid more than you think a hiring organization will spend? You worry that your current compensation will be over the organization's range for the job you seek and that an honest answer might price you out of the job.

First, be *very* sure you have current, accurate information about the pay range for this exact job at this exact organization before you make this assumption. In my experience, most of the time when people fear they're "over the range," they're wrong. Seriously. When candidates answer my money question by saying how highly paid they are—and that they're likely over the range for a role—I can almost guarantee they're *not* over the range. In fact, they're frequently below it!

Unless you know as an absolute fact that your current or recent compensation exceeds the range for a job, then simply answer honestly, as recommended above. At the appropriate time, you can add that you're open and flexible.

For example:

THEIR QUESTION: **"What are your salary requirements?"**

YOUR ANSWER: **"I most recently earned $210,000."**

THEIR RESPONSE: **"That's a bit above our range for the position."**

YOUR ANSWER: **"I respect that, and I thought that might be the case. I'm in a position right now where I can be somewhat flexible on compensation. This job doesn't require the significant travel of my previous role, and that alone has great value to me."**

THEIR RESPONSE: **"Okay, thank you. That sounds good."**

THEIR QUESTION: "What are your salary requirements?"

YOUR ANSWER: "Last year my base salary was $143,000."

THEIR RESPONSE: "That's over our current range for the position."

YOUR ANSWER: "I understand. I respect the current range that you have. Right now I'm open, compensation-wise. This job is much closer to home and that has value to me. Further, I would be eager to work with your product line."

THEIR RESPONSE: "All right, thanks."

What if your compensation has moved up and down and you'd like to get back to a higher level? That happens. You may have earned $195,000 in a prior job at ABC Inc., for example, but after a stretch out of work, you "settled" for $137,000 in your current job at XYZ Co. You'd like to get back closer to your pay at ABC. Here's how to handle that situation:

THEIR QUESTION: "What type of pay range are you looking for?"

YOUR ANSWER: "My pay in my last two positions was $137,000 and $195,000."

Note that in this instance, you include both relevant compensation numbers in your initial short answer about money. The interviewer may ask for clarification. "Which is your current salary?" "How long were you at the various pay levels?" Answer honestly.

You might not bump back up to $195,000, but letting the organization know you've been at that level will make a difference. If a specific pay level is imperative for you at this time, you might as well share it. "Right now, I want to get back to the $175,000 pay level. I believe this job has additional responsibilities compared with my current role, and it seems more in line with the work I did at ABC."

What happens if you believe your compensation is significantly lower than the job for which you're interviewing? Well, you might get a raise. On the other hand, a compensation range that is unusually low compared with other candidates could be a red flag. Why so low? Is your responsibility less than the others? Are you still learning the ropes?

One reason your compensation might be lower is if your current role is a lower level than the job you're interviewing for, but you're perceived as a candidate ready to step up to a higher level of responsibility. The interviewer might note that you're at a lower range and won't be surprised. However, you do want to prepare for an interviewer who does express surprise at the number. Again, answer honestly. Provide a bit of context if you think that would be helpful.

THEIR QUESTION: **"What are you thinking money-wise?"**

YOUR ANSWER: **"I currently earn $63,000. My pay dropped after two years out of the workforce to care for family members."**

THEIR RESPONSE: **"Great, thanks." (While thinking,** *That's below the others I've talked to. But, I understand the explanation.*)

Or

THEIR QUESTION: **"What are you thinking money-wise?"**

YOUR ANSWER: **"I currently earn $63,000."**

THEIR RESPONSE: **"Gee, that surprises me. That's lower than others we've talked to with similar experience."**

YOUR ANSWER: **"I understand. My current compensation is under market. I negotiated an agreement to work 32 hours a week so I could also manage my jewelry-import business. That business has sold, so I'm no longer in that situation."**

Or

YOUR ANSWER: **"Yes, I know the pay is on the low side. I was partly compensated in stock in the early years at the company because cash was tight."**

Or

YOUR ANSWER: **"Agreed. I'm aware that this is low when compared with similar positions. My job has had great rewards of training and growth opportunities, but I am eager to move to a higher and more competitive pay range."**

Don't—under any circumstance—bad-mouth your current or former company or complain about conditions or pay. At all times, be self-aware and positive.

The biggest money mistake you can make, under any circumstance, is to treat the money question like you're at step 10, when you're only at step 4. It's extremely off-putting for the HR team member on a phone screen, for example, to have you drill down on an exact offer, especially because 1) making an offer isn't that person's role at this point in the process, and 2) that person isn't likely to be ultimately responsible for deciding compensation. The person conducting a phone screen or early interview will likely have a sense for the range, but not be in charge of a final offer.

Similarly, later in the process, it's problematic if the hiring organization makes you an offer and you don't engage in discussing it. They say, "Here is the amount we are thinking for pay." and you answer, "Hmm. I dunno." The organization is at stage 10 and you're playing around back at stage 4. The best answer to an actual offer is to say thank you. Express your sincere gratitude. Ask for a day or two to discuss the offer with your spouse/mentor/inner circle. Promise to respond promptly. Then do so. **If you're weird about engaging in the process, you create an unnecessary issue. How much pay you might want is far less of a problem than not explicitly discussing it.**

CHAPTER 13

GETTING THE CALL

MURRAY SHUFFLED A FEW LAST PIECES OF PAPER AND CLOSED HIS FILE. He wasn't 100 percent sure about his assessment of the candidate pool for vice president of sales and marketing, but he was 90 percent there. That would have to do.

"Send me the top four to six people, Murray," Deonne had requested. "Preferably four or five." Like a lot of CEOs, she had an extremely tight schedule. She enjoyed meeting with candidates for senior-level posts but never had the time to meet with as many as she would wish to.

Murray had instructed Wynn & Zehring to fully vet the candidates and present the strongest, with the goal of inviting six or fewer for interviews on-site at Byhram Nash. He'd asked the search firm to focus on candidates most likely to match not only the job requirements (size and scope of the function, knowledge of the sector, background in e-commerce, and experience in setting sales strategy) but also leadership style and cultural fit. Based on input from Deonne and Murray, the recruitment firm had a well-nuanced definition of what staff, customers, and peers expected from the VP position.

Eager to get candidates set up with Deonne, Murray decided to call finalists himself. Scheduling meetings wasn't one of his strengths, but setting up interviews would give him an early sense of the candidates.

Thirty minutes later, all the interviews were arranged. The calls didn't go exactly as he expected. On one hand, Murray was impressed when several candidates hit the right balance of back-and-forth, speaking on-point as well as listening intently. On the other hand, one candidate launched into detailed questions far more appropriate for Deonne or an operations leader, leaving Murray feeling foolish for repeatedly needing to say, "I don't know." Two candidates asked no questions at all, despite Murray's open invitation. They surely didn't intend to appear disinterested, but that was the effect. *Better to ask questions apt for this step in the process*, Murray thought. *Couldn't they come up with something? Even basics like "Do you have any advice for me as I prepare?" or "What should I highlight during the interview?" or "What does the company most want in a new sales and marketing executive?"*

Picking up

Petra was running late, but more than glad she answered the phone. When the friendly yet professional voice on the other end introduced himself and the reason for his call, she pumped her fist in the air. An interview at Byhram Nash! The main reason Murray had called was to set up the face-to-face meeting, and Petra listened carefully to the preferred dates and times. Wednesday morning was ideal—great. She confirmed the interview length and location and double-checked who would participate in the meeting.

Murray asked Petra if she had any questions. She assumed his time was limited but also understood the value of an internal perspective. She grabbed a moment to express her gratitude for the organization's consideration of her candidacy, then asked, "What key things should I focus on as I prepare for the interview?" She listened. Took notes. Asked a clarifying question. Listened some more. After Murray paused, she thanked him and said she looked forward to the upcoming conversation.

With a week to prepare, Petra was ready to get to work. This could be a very good job, and she was committed to giving the interview her best.

CHAPTER 14

PREPARING FOR AN INTERVIEW

Part 1— Gathering Information

NO ONE CAN TELL THE WORLD ABOUT YOUR SKILLS, YOUR EXPERIENCES, AND YOUR ACCOMPLISHMENTS LIKE YOU CAN. AFTER ALL, YOU WERE THERE! And no, laying out the best of your best isn't bragging. The goal of interview preparation is to ensure you can respond to specific questions with specific answers, speaking openly, comfortably, and *accurately* about the results you've achieved at work.

A number of activities can help you get ready to talk about your skills:

- **Review your résumé**, CV, professional one-pager, bio, and the like. Highlight key activities, noting the work results most relevant to this specific position.
- **Review past job descriptions and other personnel records.** What responsibilities did you carry? What did you accomplish?
- **Consider feedback you've received throughout your career**, both formal and informal. What stands out in your performance appraisals? Any awards? What did you do that others really valued? Do you have a file

of complimentary notes and emails? (If not, start one now!)

- **Ask former colleagues and coworkers about your results.** What strikes them as most memorable? How did your individual accomplishments impact the larger organization? If you were to enlist them as job references, what would they say about your key skills and accomplishments?

- **Draft a report of your findings.** Create a summary document. Call it "My Top 10 Career Accomplishments" or "My 10 Most Amazing Skills."

You might scan those suggestions and think, *I've got that covered.* If it's been a long while since you've engaged in any of these activities, however, set aside time to catch up. You can speed the process by partnering with a career coach or résumé expert. Whatever your approach, aim to complete these basics quickly so you can turn your attention to preparing for a specific interview.

Interviewers light up when a candidate arrives well-prepared. "Did you notice she used our company acronyms?" I've heard people say. "That was impressive!" Similarly, interviewers easily spot candidates caught unprepared. "That candidate didn't know about our merger with Cuperbo & Stapley? That's three-year-old news!" "She mispronounced the name of our biggest product line!" Being prepared makes a priceless impression.

Here are some steps you can take to gather the well-rounded information you need to increase your odds of a great interview:

Know the organization

You should certainly know the basics. How large is this organization? What are its primary products or services? How is it structured? How does it compare with your prior employers? If the organization is extremely large, you might only need to educate yourself about one of its locations or divisions. Check the following sources to learn more:

- **Organization website**: Dive deep to learn how the organization presents itself and its brand. Who are its leaders? What are their backgrounds? What has the organization highlighted about recent events and trends? What's the company's messaging?
- **Online searches**: What information about the company and its products or services pops up first in search results? What else can you learn about company leaders? What news pieces or industry articles mention the organization? Has the organization won praise as a top employer? What comments do you see from raving fans or raging customers?
- **Annual reports/Forms 990:** Scan as much financial information as you can find. If you're not financially trained, ask a friend to assist. Earlier in my career, I was personally interviewing for a director role at a midsize manufacturing company. I put the company's annual report in front of a friend who had years of experience as a chief financial officer. "Is this company financially stable?" "Are there financial issues I should worry about?" The cost of lunch was well worth the guidance I received.
- **Marketing materials and social media**: Look at promotional materials produced by the organization. What's your first impression? What do you learn from the

overall look and feel? What messages and images does the organization use to sell itself? (Soft sell or hard sell? Appealing to the mind or emotions or something else?) Search for articles or white papers penned by the organization's executives. Do they show thought leadership? How does the organization strive to portray itself to external stakeholders?

- **Visit the hiring organization:** This may not always be possible, but we know of many candidates who have attended open houses, galas, or volunteer events at a hiring organization site.

- **Your network:** Leverage your professional connections to uncover organization intangibles. What's the company's reputation? How do people feel about working there? How long do they stay? Seek out employees both present and past. What do (or did) they like about working there? Why did they leave? Would they go back?

Know the job

You're probably interviewing for a specific job, so you should be familiar with that role. Do the following to make sure you're ready to answer (and ask!) questions about the job itself:

- **Job description or profile.** Study the job description, if one was provided. Read it a few times, highlighting areas where you have questions or concerns. List specific ways this job is similar to or different from other positions you have held. When you boil the document down to its most important points, what three or four major needs stand out? Scan, too, for minor details, like jargon unique to the organization.

- **Other job postings**: Compare this job description with online listings for the same job title. How is this particular one similar or different? What do those comparisons reveal about the organization, its structure, or its culture?

Know the people

You probably have the name(s) of the person (or people) who will interview you. Discover what you can about them ahead of time:

- **LinkedIn**: Look up the interviewer(s) on LinkedIn. Note career paths, tenure with the organization? How do they describe what they do? What activities and professional associations are they part of? Do you see any shared connections worth mentioning, either people, shared experiences, or interests?
- **Online information**: Do a web search of the people with whom you'll meet. What additional details show up? Service on boards of directors? Civic involvement? Articles or speaking engagements? It's all helpful background information.
- **Networking**: What does your network say about folks who work there? Do you know anyone with strong connections to people within the organization—or even to the interviewer? Searching for second- and third-degree connections via LinkedIn yields valuable information. A surprising number of executives have sparse profiles or few connections, however, so don't neglect asking around in your face-to-face network.

Back in the day when research was conducted with paper and microfiche, you could possibly get away with going into an interview relatively blank about an organization. Those days are long gone, however. The internet is exploding with information, and there's no excuse for being ill-prepared. While you don't need to have everything down about this organization before a first meeting, consider what your competitors for the position might be discovering in their own searches.

Let's say I'm presenting a candidate to a local nonprofit. I would expect the person has studied the website and knows who's on the board, and has looked at the staff to notice whether members were long-termers or new arrivals. If you're looking at a nonprofit, by golly, you'd better read its 990. How big is the organization? What are its revenue streams? If you're looking at a for-profit, have you looked at its annual report? These things don't take long. I can also promise you that looking at LinkedIn profiles is a nice touch. If you know the name of the person you're meeting with, you can build an instant connection with a comment such as "I see you attended Coe College in Iowa."

CHAPTER 15

PREPARING FOR AN INTERVIEW,

Part 2— The Job Match Matrix

YOU MIGHT BE ONE OF THOSE RARE PEOPLE WHO CAN QUICKLY RECALL EXPERIENCES, DRAW CONNECTIONS, AND EXPLAIN COMPLEX RELATIONSHIPS ON THE FLY. Most people, though, benefit from thoughtful preparation before a meeting as significant as an interview. Don't take a chance. You'll want to invest time thinking about how your past experiences connect with the particulars of this job because, throughout the interview process, you'll surely be expected to explain and illustrate the match. The second phase of your planning involves understanding and getting ready to articulate these key points.

Experts in job transition often suggest using the job description to organize your thoughts about skill and experience fit.

To begin, read through the job description provided by the hiring organization or the search professional. Read it top to bottom. Twice. Including boilerplate language. Do you understand it? Is anything unclear? Are there unfamiliar terms or insider lingo? How well do you meet the qualifications?

What are the job's core responsibilities? How about any explicit quantitative and qualitative goals? What's your gut reaction to the role? Honestly—how do you feel about your ability to do this job? Could you do the work on day one with no training? Do your past experiences equip you to do the job with a reasonable amount of training or assistance? What would you need? What onboarding would be helpful? Or would you require substantial training, coaching, and assistance to achieve success? Is this the right job for you?

Does that seem like too many questions all at once? They're just a sampling of the questions, spoken and unspoken, you'll encounter as you interview. So let's get ready.

Create a Job Match Matrix

A matrix can help capture your thoughts about how well you match a potential job. The process of filling out the matrix jogs your memory about skills and attributes relevant to the role. And the completed matrix becomes a reference as you prep for the interview.

Start with the job requirements. With the job description in hand, fill out the Qualification/Requirement column, on the left side of the matrix. For example:

Job Match Matrix

QUALIFICATION/ REQUIREMENT	MY EXPERIENCE/RESULTS
Seven years of sales management experience	
Experience with a large regional territory	
Experience selling through distribution	
Familiarity with Miller Heiman Strategic Selling Model	

	MY NARRATIVE/RATING

You might not agree the role requires all the qualifications or requirements written into the job description, but include them anyway. It's a given that the employer decided they were important enough to list.

Next, note your own background. In the center column of the Job Match Matrix, jot down your experience and results related to each qualification. What specific experiences have equipped you to do the job? What results did you achieve in each role? Any metrics you can use as evidence? Did any accomplishments earn you recognition? Your notes in this column don't require intricate detail, just enough information to be useful. Capture the highlights so that when you come back to this content in a week it still makes sense to you.

As you complete the center column, think back to *all* your relevant background, even childhood experiences or high school jobs. I once worked with a chief administration officer candidate interviewing at a large, prestigious construction company. The candidate had spent his entire career in the banking industry. The organization was willing to consider him because the position as head of administration wasn't in the core operations of the business, meaning experience in the construction industry wasn't absolutely crucial. However, during the course of interviewing, this candidate wisely wove in the detail that his father had owned a small construction company and that throughout high school and college he worked for his dad in the trades. The candidate landed the job.

For example:

Job Match Matrix

QUALIFICATION/ REQUIREMENT	MY EXPERIENCE/RESULTS
Seven years of sales management experience	· Assistant mgr, retail in college · REC-Co Sales Mgr – 2 yrs · Promoted from within · Performance rating of "superior" · Paqpro Regional Sales Lead – 4 yrs · Promoted from within
Experience with a large regional territory	· REC-Co five state area · Paqpro ten state region
Experience selling through distribution	· REC-Co sold direct · Paqpro-sold through distribution, but not my division · Helped the co. review possible distributor model for my division
Familiarity with Miller Heiman Strategic Selling Model	· Have taken 3-sales excellence and 2-sales manager training courses through Univ professional ed program · Selected to get the management training by being voted "Future leader program" · Paqpro internal courses on customer management · Paqpro training on how to coach staff

MY NARRATIVE/RATING

Next, use the remaining column to add your narrative and rating. This information fills the experiences you noted in the center column with life and meaning. What else is important to communicate about your qualifications in a specific area? A particular story or achievement of note? Any recognition or awards? Did you overcome any unusual challenges? What were the extenuating circumstances? Don't make your notes too lengthy, and certainly *do not memorize* the narrative information. Simply get it down. Your narrative comments can be useful reminders for review prior to the interview.

Lastly, in the remaining column, rate yourself. High (H), medium (M), or low (L) is specific enough. My rule: You *must* have at least one high, one medium, *and* one low. That will ensure you have a balanced assessment of yourself relative to the role. While you might indeed be a great fit for this position, not everything in your background will be precisely what the hiring company wants. Force yourself to evaluate which areas appear to be the strongest match and which do not.

Job Match Matrix

QUALIFICATION/ REQUIREMENT	MY EXPERIENCE/RESULTS
Seven years of sales management experience	· Assistant mgr, retail in college · REC-Co Sales Mgr – 2 yrs · Promoted from within · Performance rating of "superior" · Paqpro Regional Sales Lead – 4 yrs · Promoted from within
Experience with a large regional territory	· REC-Co five state area · Paqpro ten state region
Experience selling through distribution	· REC-Co sold direct · Paqpro-sold through distribution, but not my division · Helped the co. review possible distributor model for my division
Familiarity with Miller Heiman Strategic Selling Model	· Have taken 3-sales excellence and 2-sales manager training courses through Univ professional ed program · Selected to get the management training by being voted "Future leader program" · Paqpro internal courses on customer management · Paqpro training on how to coach staff

MY NARRATIVE/RATING
• 6 years of total sales management, 3 years retail management, a good mix of responsibility • Different expectations of manager role in the two companies, learned two models for sales manager • Think I am a "natural manager" • Good feedback from others, including staff and bosses – note comments from Jon and Kao **RATING:** Med
• All experience is in regional sales orgs • Regions of 5 – 10 states average for these industries • Seek to work in larger regions • I'm an "Army brat" and very used to travel and different places **RATING:** Med
• Have sold only direct • Peers sold throughdistribution • Learned a bit about it from them • Interested to learn more; this is my career direction • Disappointed, not implemented in my division at Paqpro **RATING:** Low
• I like training and have taken several courses • Familiar with sales models and applying them (example of winning a big account with the BestSell model, president's reaction!) • Read a lot of sales books, listen to sales-technique CDs in car (including Miller Heiman) but haven't taken the course **RATING:** Med

I've included a blank Job Match Matrix at the back of the book. Use this process every time you're getting ready for an important interview. And don't forget these rules:

- For the Qualification/Requirement column, use the job description as your template.
- Honor the qualifications and requirements specified by the employer. Don't change or exclude them, even if you mightily disagree with some.
- In the My Experience/Results column, jot down related background in each area, highlighting results you achieved for each point. Be thorough without being exhaustive.
- In the My Narrative/Rating column, add color to your experiences and results. Include stories only if they are absolutely relevant and will be meaningful in the context of an interview.
- As you rate yourself, force yourself to include at least one high, one medium, and one low rating.
- Do not, under any circumstances, memorize the information on your matrix. In an interview, natural delivery beats canned responses every day of the week. And if you don't remember every single point, so be it. Perhaps you will have an opportunity to mention additional detail in a subsequent communication.

Be authentic and be honest. You're on your way to a great interview!

How do you know when you've prepared *enough*? You should know enough to have a general discussion about the company, the position, and how your background relates (and how it doesn't).

Make sure your preparation time and your strategy are proportional. Too often, I hear of candidates spending mega-hours researching the company and not enough time looking at the position and coming up with background examples that align with the position. Keep in mind that the interviewer will ask mostly about you—and perhaps only a few questions about what you know about the company. Make sure your prep time is spent proportionally. You need to know enough to draw connections, not to win a corporate trivia quiz.

Generating relevant and insightful questions

As you work through the Job Match Matrix, questions about the role and organization will undoubtedly come to mind. Some of the best questions arise when you're interacting with the role itself (in this case, a job description) rather than thinking about the job in the abstract. Why? Those questions point toward what the company needs and not just what you want from a job. They will enliven your conversations and help create the back-and-forth that both sides feel contributes to an excellent interview.

Go to each interview prepared with questions *appropriate to where you are in the interview process.* Keep in mind that your level of preparation for each interview stage should deepen the further you go into the process. Think of the recruitment process like a funnel: The further you go, the narrower it becomes. It would seem strange, for example, to ask in a first interview if the organization offers a company-paid cell-phone plan. It would be equally strange to ask in a final interview, "So, how does the company sell its products?"

Go to each interview prepared with questions *appropriate for the person you're meeting.* The human resources director, for example, would be the right person to ask about the benefits plan. The vice president of strategic operations would be a good resource for information about international expansion plans.

Be sure to understand how the interviewer's role relates to the job you're being considered for. Each interviewer has a unique interest in what the candidate brings to the table and therefore may tailor questions accordingly. If you meet with people who will report to you, for example, they may be interested in probing your leadership and management styles and how you engage employees or handle employee-relations challenges. If an interviewer is a cross-disciplinary peer, then the core of that person's questions may be about your collaboration skills, style, and ability to partner.

Likewise, at least some of your questions should reflect your day-to-day interactions with the roles of your interviewers. They need to experience how you engage at a practical, personal level. It's all about the Monday Morning Staff Meeting, right?

CHAPTER 16

HOW *NOT* TO PREPARE

THERE COMES A POINT WHERE PREPAREDNESS TURNS INTO A LIABILITY. Let me tell you what you're *not* aiming to do.

Candidates, in an effort to appear prepared, sometimes come to the interview with specific stories about themselves they feel they *must* share. Or they bring handouts or other items to showcase in the meeting—and then look for ways to wedge these extras into the interview conversation whether they fit or not. While that type of preparation isn't necessarily bad, it can lead to trouble.

I've had candidates ask if they should prepare a slide deck of a business case demonstrating how they'll solve all the prospective employer's problems. That's a high-risk, high-reward proposition. It's potentially high-reward because your assumptions might be accurate, and by articulating an outline of a high-level business plan, you could position yourself as a strategic thinker and a crucial part of a solution. It also sheds light on how you tackle a business problem. However, it's also high-risk because, as an outsider, you're likely basing the business case on assumptions about what the employer needs. Assume wrong, and you could come across as presumptuous or miss the mark badly. In my experience, the risk greatly outweighs the potential reward.

Being overprepared can be as troublesome as being underprepared. The spot where preparation is "just right" is when your preparation equips you for a nice dialogue. Interviewers think, *Clearly, you understand what we do here.* You come across as knowledgeable and articulate.

Now, there are times when your interviewers want specific stories. Your cue is a behavioral question that starts with "Tell me about a time when" or something similar, like "Tell me about a time when you developed one of your staff."

"Okay," you could say in response. "I use an approach that starts with the performance appraisal and collaborative goal setting. When I met with Ryan, we really targeted his team-building skills. He had some significant communication deficits, along with natural leadership potential. Over the course of a few years, we laid out classes, coaching, and assignments. The result was that Ryan got promoted and now oversees 25 people."

Notice that the answer was more than a bland and incomplete "I'm really good at developing people. It's one of the most important jobs about a leader. At the end of the day, you're only as good as the investment you've made in your staff." The vignette could have been about Ryan or anyone else you've successfully developed. But interviewers want a real-life example, and if you can't provide one, it sounds like you lack either self-awareness or observable results.

If you're trying to prepare for these behavioral questions, the best approach is to jot down an example or two, a "for instance," the kind of notes you generated in the Job Match Matrix.

However, don't go so far as to write out a story, read it, rehearse it, and commit it to memory. Just have it in mind: *I'm going to tell the story about Ryan. I want it to come off natural and in the moment.*

If you've been through job-transition coaching, you might have learned a storytelling formula like SAR (situation, action, result) or PAR (problem, action, result). While

I appreciate that those formulas call out helpful elements of an effective story, I also think you're at risk of sabotaging your chances in an interview as soon as the formula causes you to sound formulaic. **Just have that "for instance" in mind, and tell your story as if you lived it (which you did!).**

> **Your goal in responding to these "tell me about a time when" questions is to provide answers that are *specific* but not *canned*.** Most of us aren't particularly good at memorizing something on Tuesday and then being off the cuff on Wednesday. If we've rehearsed a story to death on Tuesday, on Wednesday we're going to sound stilted. Employers want to hire someone who listens to a question and responds, not someone who uses a question as a chance to slide in a prepackaged story.

> At an executive-level interview, it's important to demonstrate your ability to respond in the moment, not regurgitate a script. After all, "on your feet" thinking is a daily requirement of any executive role.

More often than not, I cringe when candidates start to tell stories. Why? People who win the interview are authentic.

CHAPTER 17

ARRIVING FOR THE INTERVIEW

PETRA BEGAY REACHED INTO HER BRIEFCASE AND SWITCHED HER CELL PHONE TO SILENT, relieved she hadn't forgotten that all-important detail before the start of her interview. Last month she'd attended a funeral where a phone's loud ringing disrupted the somber eulogy. She'd felt embarrassed for the culprit—but wow, a funeral?

The lobby at Byhram Nash was windowed and bright, nicely accenting leather seating in a cool color scheme. Recently redecorated? Petra had reviewed the company's financials and noticed the company had enjoyed years of strong sales, but things appeared to be slowing as of late. New manufacturing facilities were suffering cost overruns. Something to be concerned about?

Speaking of concerns, the Byhram Nash CEO was fairly new in her position, wasn't she? Petra wasn't at all sure she'd be comfortable with an unproven executive, but she told herself to settle back a bit. She had lots of questions, but that's why she was here, right? This first face-to-face meeting was a chance to learn more about the company and its direction as well as to start getting to know the CEO. Petra knew there would be more meetings after this, if everyone remained interested.

When executive recruiter Nick Wyatt initially called

about this job, Petra told him no. Graciously, of course, but a firm decline nonetheless. At that time, Petra was riding a long surge of success at her firm, and her firm's board had signaled that she would likely succeed the current chief operating officer when he retired. She'd even been granted a $10,000 stipend to spend on leadership training and coaching to prepare her for the role.

The second time Nick Wyatt called, Petra took a few more minutes to listen. The conversation actually helped Petra reflect on her career goals and nudged her to pursue this opportunity. She learned more and became intrigued. Well, one thing had led to another, and now here she was, waiting in the lobby for an interview with the top leader of Byhram Nash.

Glancing up from her chair in the lobby, Petra was surprised to see Deonne Bratt Pennington herself enter the room. That seemed less formal and more welcoming than other organizations she'd met with.

Petra stood and extended her hand in response to Deonne's greeting. "Good morning, Ms. Pennington. It's an honor to meet you."

Deonne replied with a greeting and turned to thank the front desk associate. "Please, call me Deonne." Petra straightened her back, smiled, and nodded. "Did you have trouble finding our office?"

No—no trouble. Petra had long been familiar with Byhram Nash and its locations. And she'd taken an oil-painting course nearby.

Petra mentioned that fact, and as Deonne led her to a conference room off the lobby the two talked about the local arts scene. Petra accepted a glass of water and Deonne set her folder down on the table.

"Where would you like me to sit?" asked Petra.

"Across the table, there," directed Deonne, and Petra happily complied. "I'm delighted to have you here today, Petra."

Petra settled into her chair. ***We appear to be off to a good start***, she thought.

CHAPTER 18

MAKE AN EXECUTIVE IMPRESSION

PROSPECTIVE EMPLOYERS SHOULD KNOW YOU'RE AN ACCOMPLISHED EXECUTIVE SIMPLY BY HOW YOU CARRY YOURSELF, EVEN BEFORE YOU SAY A WORD. If you overdo it, however, you can unintentionally come across as arrogant. Quiet, unassuming confidence is the key—an openness and warmth that draws people in. It gives hiring executives a positive first impression, makes them interested in what you have to say, and leaves them wanting more.

Candidates anticipate, research, plan, and prepare for interviews, even to the point of standing in front of a mirror to practice answers. But the unspoken way you carry yourself also impacts your success. Some call it executive presence. While outright bravado or cockiness can be a deal breaker right from the start, an authentic confidence that flows from knowing who you are and who you're not is a winning trait.

We've all encountered people who ooze this presence. As we meet and interact with them, we say to ourselves, "Wow, they have it all together!" Executive presence has an aura of subtle humility that comes from being comfortable in your own skin. It telegraphs an approachability that says to the world, "I'm confident in who I am and what I say. I also respect you and want to hear you, too. Tell me more."

Executive presence communicates depth and substance. I'm intentionally not calling this characteristic "charisma," because that word can connote superficial flashiness and insincerity.

In really practical terms, executive presence shows at an interview when you get to the core of questions quickly and concisely. The more you go on and on, the less impactful you are. (Frankly, you're actually less believable.) When you possess executive presence, the words you're saying naturally align with your nonverbal signals. If you're asked about something you're proud of, for example, your voice and facial expressions demonstrate consistency with your response. You smile and your voice conveys excitement; after all, this is a positive thing you're talking about. It's like when parents talk (brag!) about their kids. They're grinning and animated. Does that congruence between your verbal and nonverbal responses ring out when you interview?

First impressions

Executive presence is just one part of making a solid first impression. Much research underscores the power of a positive first impression, and while good executive presence contributes, it is a separate thing to mind and work on.

If you're able to give the interviewer a positive first impression, you start off on a good foot with the interviewer fully engaged. So your first job in those early moments is to foster and maintain that positive impression. By the way, from experience I absolutely agree with the axiom that interviewers often decide if they like you within the first few minutes. Make a less-than-favorable first impression, and you'll have to work two or three times as hard to recapture your audience.

NOTE THESE EASY REMINDERS ON MAKING A POSITIVE FIRST IMPRESSION:

☐ **SHOW UP ON TIME.** Have your contact's phone number with you and call if you get delayed. But quite honestly, it's tough to recover if you're late. People's calendars are tight. Tardiness is disrespectful. Plan ahead. Take a test run to the interview location, traveling at the same time of day so you can anticipate traffic. Scope out a place to park, especially if you have to walk or need to park at a meter. I don't recommend relying on GPS. It isn't 100 percent accurate and getting lost is inexcusable.

Having said that, if the worst happens and you're late, make the best of it. I once had a candidate for a library director role go to the wrong interview location—and she had taken the bus! We connected by phone and I redirected her to the correct location. It was cold and rainy, but she hopped the next bus to the right spot and was there within a half hour. The interview committee used the extra time to have a mini meeting on another topic and they weren't put out at all. The candidate apologized but did not let the situation get her down. She put on her game face and did a nice job in the interview.

☐ **LOOK PUT TOGETHER.** Bring a portfolio with fresh copies of your résumé, a memo tablet, and a pen. While some people tuck a cheat sheet of notes and questions into that nice portfolio, remember that the less you need to rely on written prompts at the executive level, the more professional you will appear.

☐ **DRESS THE PART.** It matters! Shined shoes, matching socks, well-fitting and seasonably appropriate clothes. If you haven't interviewed in a while, invest in current interviewing attire. Given the shift to business casual, your everyday work wardrobe might not be appropriate, even if you're a seasoned executive. I was recently interviewing a candidate and caught a glimpse of something shiny on his sleeve. A closer look revealed he had stapled his cuff, which inevitably came loose. I understand that he may have been in a pinch, but it *was* a distraction.

☐ **MAKE EYE CONTACT.** For heaven's sake, look people in the eye! I can't be any more straightforward than that. Eye contact engages your listener. And while excellent eye contact will rarely be consciously noted, poor eye contact will rarely be overlooked.

A distant cousin was a candidate for a senior government position. She was exceptionally well-qualified and passionate about the role. After the first interview, she was informed she wouldn't be invited back, news that left her sorely disappointed. The feedback from the recruiter? "Lacked eye contact!"

Granted, this is a simple skill most of us have mastered and rarely need to think about. However, even good habits can easily come undone from the stress of interviewing or discomfort with the people involved.

If your natural tendency is to look away when thinking, that's okay. Just be sure to reengage the interviewer when actually answering. The importance of eye contact multiplies during group interviews. You'll keep interviewers interested by regularly meeting the gaze of each person present.

☐ **SMILE.** Sound silly? I've met executives with infectious smiles who are determined to look like "an executive," so much so that their serious facial expressions appear cold and inhuman. And in moments of nervousness, any of us can lose our smile. But smiles warm up the room and move your interviewers from forming a pleasant first impression of you to actually liking you.

It isn't hard to fathom what goes through a hiring executive's mind, and yet it's too often forgotten: Will everyone like this addition to our team? Will she connect and cooperate with team members? How will our customers respond? Will the person be pleasant for *me* to work with, or will he drive me crazy?

This is the Monday Morning Staff Meeting factor—that interviewers *like* you and begin to visualize you at a seat in *their* company, not in your former company. The interview process is all about making that translation.

CHAPTER 19

AT THE INTERVIEW

FROM MURRAY'S PERSPECTIVE, PICKING TOP CANDIDATES FOR HIS CEO TO INTERVIEW PROVED MORE DIFFICULT THAN HE INITIALLY THOUGHT IT WOULD. Wynn & Zehring had brought him a slate of the maximum six candidates Deonne had requested, but he still had to put his professional stamp of approval on the choices. After all, this was a critical top-level hire. To him, there was little room for error. His credibility as head of human resources would rise or fall with this hire.

Throughout the process, Murray had worried about how a candidate would match not just the job description but also the organization. What can you really tell about someone from a résumé and a phone conversation?

As it turned out, Murray concluded, plenty. He reminded himself that these candidates had been vetted by the executive search firm. People with intimate knowledge of the job description, including the external recruiters and Murray himself, had reviewed the candidates' professional experiences and compared those experiences with the skills needed by the next vice president of sales and marketing.

All the candidates who moved forward to face-to-face interviews with Deonne could, on paper, perform the tasks of the job. All of them had the appropriate length and level of experience. None had worked for organizations deemed any less sophisticated than Byhram Nash. In her interviews, Deonne would quickly reaffirm the qualifications, then expend the bulk of her energy determining which person would be the best fit for the organization, for the leadership team, and for her.

Once Deonne settled into her chair across the interview table from Petra Begay, everyone's hard work of moving candidates forward was on the line. "Petra," Deonne began, "I've done my homework on you and your background. But I'd love to get to know you firsthand. Tell me about yourself."

CHAPTER 20

A DOZEN ESSENTIAL INTERVIEW TIPS

PICTURE YOURSELF AS PETRA, SITTING ACROSS THE TABLE FROM THE CEO AT A FACE-TO-FACE INTERVIEW. You' ve reviewed the job description countless times, picking it apart point by point, noting where your background is a match with each requirement. On the points where your background is less strong, you feel comfortable explaining what level of match is there.

You've survived phone screens and vetting interviews, and at each step your candidacy for a highly desirable executive role has moved forward. By now, you're thoroughly steeped in the organization and started to feel connections with the people you've met along the way.

You're determined not to blow this opportunity. You want this job. Maybe you're at the point in your job search where you truly need to win the interview. As you reach a point where you worry you'll burst with anxiety and anticipation, the CEO asks the first question.

How will you perform in this moment? What interviewing practices will ensure you take your best shot? As I said at the start, **your ability to interview well has a direct impact on whether you land the job you want.** You know that interviewing well doesn't just involve describing your match to a position description; it also means demonstrating your fit within an organization.

You've done ample preparation to get to this point. Now let me share a dozen tips that capture the best interview practices I've seen—behaviors that bring results. When we've finished these tips, more help will follow, I promise, including tips at the end of this book on answering a dozen common and challenging interview questions. (Spoiler alert: Sometimes they're the same thing!)

There's no magic guarantee with any answer, and I can't teach you a secret handshake that always results in a job offer. **But I will offer advice based on patterns I've observed in literally thousands of interviews, whether I'm asking the questions or watching organizational leaders query candidates, draw conclusions, and finalize hiring decisions.**

Here we go.

➔ TIP 1: START WITH CONFIDENCE IN YOUR SKILLS

You want to enter the interview confident in the range and depth of skills you possess. As much as I emphasize that the hiring organization is looking for fit (in part because candidates so rarely hear that indisputable truth), the hiring organization also needs to feel entirely comfortable that you can do the job. Therefore, you shouldn't hesitate to come with a confident style about the things you absolutely do well. *Confidence, not arrogance*. Imagine yourself on the other side of the table. As the interviewer, what would make ***you*** comfortable about the candidate's abilities?

If you're certain you can do this job (or the part of the job under discussion), go ahead and say so. Adding context to your statement is even better (I'll share more on context in tip 6). For example, "Every company is different, of course, but I've taken two organizations and four divisions through the lean manufacturing process. I'm confident I can do the same at this company." Or "I know that your organization will have some nuances, but I'm a five-year veteran in this type of printed-coating product line. I'm entirely comfortable I can do the design work required in this job."

As I've said before, the fact that you've been invited to an interview means it's highly likely your skills are a match for the job. If you're an elementary school principal, you're probably not applying to be the marketing manager of new-product development at a medical-device manufacturer, or vice versa. And even if you did apply, you wouldn't likely be asked to interview. The position you seek might be a bit of a stretch, but I trust you're not reaching unreasonably beyond your skills.

> **Virtually all interviews will include questions related to skills and abilities, and your work on the Job Match Matrix prepares you to answer. But I need to point out a common failure I observe when candidates describe their skills: When you're asked about your skills, talk about your skills.**

Don't confuse skills with style. I often hear interviewers ask about a candidate's skills and abilities only to get an answer that relates to style. Here's an example:

INTERVIEWER QUESTION: "Can you talk about how you would assess your strongest product-development skills with regard to the role of senior research chemist?"

ANSWER: "Well, I'm first and foremost a team player. I'm good at collaborating and I enjoy group decision-making."

The content of the answer might be true, but it doesn't answer the question—which is about your *skills*. Failing to answer a skill question with a skill answer calls into doubt whether you have what it takes. There will likely be questions about your work style later in the interview. So answer questions about skills with facts and examples about your skills. Conversely, answer questions about style with information and examples that describe your style. If you're not tracking with what I'm saying, consider this: **Skill is about what you can do. Style is about how you do it.**

➜ TIP 2: BE HONEST ABOUT YOUR DEVELOPMENT AREAS

While we're on the topic of skills, I'm going to jump right to a related point. **This next step isn't easy, but you need to be square with interviewers about skill areas that aren't your top strengths, or even areas that still might be considered weaknesses.** Again, think back to constructive feedback you've received in the past. Read your performance reviews afresh if you have those documents at hand, studying the developmental points you might have glossed over as you put together your résumé or created a Job Match Matrix. Where are your gaps? What are you currently working on? What changes—new discoveries, techniques, or strategies—have occurred in your field or industry that you still need to master?

Although you'll impress interviewers with a quiet confidence about areas where you excel, you will always make a better impression when you show awareness of areas where you're less strong. Consider the following example from a recent interview:

INTERVIEWER QUESTION: "Are there any areas where you might need training or onboarding assistance to get up to speed in this job?"

CANDIDATE 1 ANSWER: "No, I can't think of anything. I believe I could do it all."

You may think this is a fine answer. You might believe it builds credibility with the interviewer. After all, who wouldn't want to hire someone who can "do it all"?

Counterintuitively, perhaps, it doesn't. The interviewer has probably never met anyone 100 percent optimally prepared for a new role. Such a person doesn't exist in the real world. How could someone realistically claim to "know it all" or "do it all," especially during an interview? This claim simply doesn't ring true; sometimes we don't know what we don't know. In this true example, the group of interviewers decided to pass on the candidate in part because that person couldn't think of anything that required extra training or onboarding.

Consider the following better answers by other candidates for the same job:

CANDIDATE 2 ANSWER: "I do believe that my skills are a strong resource for this role as I understand it. But my most recent work in Colorado real estate law goes back four years. I'd want to shore up my knowledge, particularly regarding any recent changes in the laws."

What if you seriously believe you can do the job effectively right out of the gate? Or what if you can't think of a meaningful deficiency in the moment? Then offer this honest answer: "Every new job brings things to learn." The new organization might have tightly prescribed processes. Its product-development cycle could look different from what you're used to. The new company might work globally, while your current organization shines closer to home. Your fallback answer to this question is to acknowledge the uniqueness of the new organization and any new knowledge areas or work patterns you would need to learn.

> **CANDIDATE 3 ANSWER:** "I feel my skills and background are a good match for the role, and I can't think of a significant skill gap right now. However, I do know I'll need to get up to speed on the nuances of working with health care providers as clients, versus working with health care software manufacturers. I know there will be differences. And my current territory covers the northern United States. Working the Toronto region would be new as well."

> **CANDIDATE 4 ANSWER:** "I believe my skills and experiences are a good match for the position, and I can't think of any major skill gaps right now. However, every organization has its own culture and way of doing things. I'd need to get up to speed on the nuances of how you work together and with customers."

The best answers about your lesser skills, development areas, or gaping holes are honest and authentic. Don't pretend you're more qualified or more of a fit than you are. Don't oversell. Don't ever make up capabilities or expertise you don't possess. Even if you think you've won the moment, you're likely to lose in the long run. Organizations want to hire real human beings, and real people are never perfect.

➔ TIP 3: LISTEN WELL

You're likely thinking: "I'm a good listener!" I've never met an executive who didn't make that claim. Yet only a small percentage of candidates exhibit truly great listening *in the context of job interviews.* What a missed opportunity!

When I debrief my organizational clients after their interviews with a slate of candidates, they sometimes remark that one or another lacked listening skills. But when I search my interview notes (taken, of course, from the back of the room as I observed firsthand), I find the candidate invariably *said* something along the way about being a skilled listener. Come to think of it, I've never had a candidate claim to be a poor or even average listener. So why are plenty of interviewees rated by client organizations as poor listeners? What's up?

You might assume your overall objective at an interview is to talk, but your first task is actually to listen well. As a poor listener, what you communicate to the interviewer is this: "What *I* say is more important than what *you* say" or "I really don't have much to learn from this conversation with you."

As a good listener, you convey to the interviewer that "I value what you're saying" and "I want to thoroughly understand your perspective" and "What we're talking about is truly important!" Being a good listener sends the message that other points of view matter to you and that you're open to considering their merits, which is a core attribute organizations want when building a leadership team.

True active listening goes beyond not interrupting. It means not formulating your own answer in your head while the interviewer is talking. Good, active listeners also follow up with clarifying questions, and everything from their body language to the focus of their gaze communicates genuine interest.

Want to know one of the most egregious examples of bad listening? It's missing or ignoring the clues embedded in interview questions.

As in the question, "Can you give us two examples of that?"

The speaker asked for two examples. Not one. Not three.

This might sound overly simplistic, but I can assure you that at least *half* of all interviewees miss these amazingly straightforward cues, with the result that they neglect what the interviewer really wants to know, and go in their own direction. What does that communicate? It *shouts*, "I'm not listening!" Or "I don't care what you want. I'll do what *I* want!"

If you have a good reason for wanting to respond differently from what's asked, check with the interviewer. Ask, "May I give one example with two components?" Or "I can think of several things; may I offer three examples?" The interviewer will appreciate the request and will virtually always approve.

By responding to interviewers' cues, you let them know you heard and understood. You demonstrate that you honor the question and want to do it the best justice you can.

Do you notice the difference?

Your role (especially early in the process) is to be an information provider, and I suppose, also a follower. Toward the end of a process, you'll likely have a chance to lead a bit of the conversation. Even then, do it only for a bit.

Let's look at a couple of questions with embedded clues:

INTERVIEWER QUESTION: "Could you talk about your earliest big sale and what you learned from it?"

ANSWER: The questioner wants to hear about an experience from early in your career. The questioner also wants to see how you learned lessons at that stage. So your answer would accomplish these things:

- Tell about a big sale you achieved **early** in your career.
- Explain what you **learned** from that situation.

INTERVIEWER QUESTION: "Could you talk about the typical way you handle employee performance issues—and describe the toughest situation you've dealt with? Have you changed your approach over the years?"

ANSWER: Try these:

- Talk about your usual method for responding to employee performance issues (not your *beliefs* or your *philosophy* but the actual *methods* or *steps* you use).
- Recount a tough performance issue (ideally a fairly recent example).
- Describe how your style has or hasn't evolved over the years.

Does this all seem ridiculously obvious? Good! Then you will be aware and ready to catch and respond to clues such as these:

- When an interviewer asks for "an example," give ONE.
- When an interviewer asks for "a couple of examples," give TWO.
- When an interviewer asks for "a few examples," give TWO or THREE.
- When the interviewer asks for a "quick overview," make your answer SHORT.
- When the interviewer asks for "a detailed explanation," make your answer LONGER.

As a college instructor, I always told my students to carefully read the assignment. ("Read the instructions three times before starting," I would admonish.) The instruction sheet invariably held many clues explaining exactly what I wanted. I allowed some flexibility, of course, but key parameters were always in the instructions. The same principle applies to interviews. Miss the instructions, and you won't score a top grade.

➜ TIP 4: LEVERAGE SILENCE

You might feel a natural urge to keep talking during an interview, filling empty air rather than let a conversation seemingly stall. Resist the urge! Silence is okay when you need a moment to gather your thoughts before you begin a response. Silence is more than okay when you've finished answering a question!

When you have completed your thought, just stop. It takes others a second to register that you've finished your answer. It takes another for them to begin asking their next question. They might be pondering whether they wish to ask a follow-up question. They may need to look down at their notes to see what's next. They might be deciding to change the order of things. During that brief pause after your answer, there may be silence. That's good. Make the most of it. Breathe easy. Sit calmly.

Silence is golden. Whatever you do, *don't* jump in and fill it with more talk. Resist the urge to interject. Silence is normal and even necessary to the interview.

➔ TIP 5: ANSWER THE QUESTION!

You must answer each question posed to you to the best of your ability, or defer the question if you need more time to consider your response. Avoiding a difficult question never works.

Not long ago I had a memorable encounter with a candidate for a role as an organizational president. Although the job was out of state, my interview with this local candidate was booked at my office in Minneapolis. In a telephone screen I had conducted myself, the candidate clearly stated his openness to relocating to my client's headquarters in another region. (Remember those feasibility questions that get asked right away in the process?)

On the day of the interview, the candidate showed up wearing jeans, apologetic for his casual attire. "Whew!" he said. "I've been busy all day unpacking my house." Another moving van was scheduled to arrive later that day. "Even moving just a few miles is a big hassle!" he exclaimed.

Given our prior conversations, I was startled. This gentleman had appeared highly interested in the job. Considering his current move, I started the interview by asking about his ability to relocate to our client's headquarters. Well, clearly this was a question the candidate didn't wish to answer directly. Perhaps he thought he could work remotely. But rather than tackling the issue head-on as he should have, he talked about everything *other* than the question I had asked. Twenty minutes of stories! His response was a litany of connected episodes, one after the other with no break for me to jump in.

When I finally squeezed a word in, I reasked the question, albeit a bit differently. I asked whether he was indeed interested in this job as a full-time position requiring relocation, or if he was only considering a commuting or consulting arrangement. Clearly, he didn't want to answer that question either. Twenty more minutes and multiple stories later, I *still* didn't have an answer.

A few minutes into this interaction I knew I couldn't put this candidate in front of my client. His question-avoiding behavior was inappropriate and unacceptable. I'm open to discussing most options, but here was an issue that had to be settled.

If you fear specific topics or questions, seek assistance in thinking how to professionally put issues on the table for a positive discussion. Lean on a mentor, a former colleague, or a coach. Never tell yourself you can choose to shut out any sensitive questions or topics.

Similarly, if your background contains details that could hurt your candidacy, take initiative and raise the topic right away. Recruiters will likely find out anyway through an online search or other avenues used to research candidates. Don't put anyone in the hiring process in a position of having to later discover unfavorable facts about you, perhaps during a pre-employment background check. Your cover-up might well be perceived less kindly than whatever surprise emerges.

I had a candidate who had served as chief investment officer at a company that suffered a public downturn. The story was all over the media, with his name sprinkled throughout. We chose a strategy of addressing this early in the search process by raising his role in the situation and detailing what he would do differently next time around. Although this candidate's first inclination was to wait to see if the issue came up, I advised him to demonstrate integrity and take the lead, putting everything on the table both with the recruiter and prospective employer. In the end, an unfortunate episode that could have been a severe mark against his candidacy came across with positive impact.

➜ TIP 6: PROVIDE CONTEXT FOR YOUR ACCOMPLISHMENTS.

A recent search I conducted reminded me why providing context is crucial. Two competing candidates brought similar backgrounds as they vied for the CEO role at a civic organization. One candidate skillfully helped the board of directors see how his experience related to the open position by connecting specific points of his work history with specific job requirements. He provided clear comparisons and contrasts, helping the board easily *see* the relevance of his experience. He used statements like these:

> "My organization has up to 20 state and county government contracts under management at any one time. I understand your organization has a similar number."

> "We recently added a facility in the northern part of the state to meet the needs of an underserved population. This relates to what I understand your organization is considering with the mobile rural-service program."

While the other candidate could list similar work experience, she failed to do so, and failed to match her experience to the current needs of the organization. By not providing context, she left it to board members to judge relevance. They judged in favor of the other candidate.

There's no guarantee your interviewers will draw the right conclusions about the relevance of your work history if you don't make the connections for them.

Put yourself in the shoes of the person you're meeting with. Interviews are inherently disjointed affairs. With many topics to cover, the questioner often jumps around to cover everything. Furthermore, if you're among a pool of candidates, the amount of data presented to a hiring team from résumés, candidate summaries, assessments, and the like can be overwhelming. Even questioners who have amazing recall or read along in your résumé as you interview might miss connections that appear obvious to you.

It's your responsibility to convey not just your achievements and expertise but the direct application of that experience to this employer. You may have a mental list of accomplishments you want to convey, examples you want to share, and successes you want to tout, but don't neglect to convey how those experiences *directly pertain to the job or company*. Assume that connecting the dots is up to you.

You need to own your claims. I've found interview answers aren't as effective when spoken from the perspective of the generic "you." These claims feel disconnected from your real-life experience and, therefore, less relevant and impactful. For example, consider the difference in the following two answers:

QUESTION: "This position requires significant public speaking. What kinds of presentations do you give, and how do you prepare?

ANSWER A: "You know, in these types of jobs, you present a lot to various groups. Before each presentation, you need to think about the audience. You should even see if you can talk with some potential audience members to get their perspectives, asking them about any concerns or issues you might face. Then you need to rehearse and prepare."

Versus:

ANSWER B: "You know, in my job, I present a lot to various groups. Before each presentation, I think about the audience. I even like to talk with potential audience members to get their perspectives, asking them about any concerns I might face. Then I rehearse and revise."

Do you hear the difference? The first answer sounds suggestive, as "What *could* a person do?" or "What *might* a person do?" The second answer expresses what the candidate ***actually does.***

When asked a direct question about you—your thinking process, planning process, execution of work—your answer should be equally direct. Don't hesitate to share your exact process or approach. Talk about what *you* do. Don't water down the answer with indirect references. The interviewer is trying to visualize you in the job. Help achieve that with clear answers about ***you.***

➜ TIP 7: EMPHASIZE SPECIFICS ABOUT WHAT YOU DO WELL

You tell me: Which statement is more persuasive? 1) "I'm a natural salesperson and I'm good!" or 2) "I've earned a Top 10 Percent sales honor each of the last five years." Or how about this: 1) "I've been well-trained in the sales process," or 2) "I've been certified in the Miller Heiman Strategic Selling model. I've also taken the Level I and Level II training in the Five-Point Sales methodology."

Specific is always better than general. Unless an interviewer explicitly asks for a "high-level view" or a "general opinion" or similar, you're better off with specific examples.

In response to a question about experience with mentoring, for example, you might give this general answer: "I really believe in mentoring. I try to mentor others and have made it a habit for years. It's crucial to me to develop talent on my team."

Sound good? Maybe. But not as good as this: "I believe so strongly in mentoring that I consistently build in mentoring activities for my staff. Every year, for example, each staff member and I decide on a professional development plan that focuses his or her growth in a couple of areas. That might include classes or experiential learning, and I make sure we include a role for me in helping the staff member develop—in other words, mentoring. Often, this means checking in over lunch once a month. I've had excellent results from this approach. In just the last two years, three members of my staff have been promoted to higher positions in our company. And we still hold our monthly lunches!"

The temptation to reply in interviews with generalities or to wax philosophical often shows up in discussions of soft skills like leadership, communication, or teamwork. Everyone believes in their importance. In all my years of search, I've never had a candidate say, "I'm a micromanager with a closed-door policy." When candidates talk about their past or present bosses or peers, however, I often hear descriptions like "closed door/unavailable" or "too hands-on." Hmmm.

Let's look at some examples of what works and what doesn't:

LESS SPECIFIC, LESS EFFECTIVE

- "I'm a people person. I love working with others."
- "I'm dedicated to the profession of architecture. I have been for years."
- "I get results. You could call me a 'rock star' achiever."

MORE SPECIFIC, MORE EFFECTIVE

- "I'm a people person. I start every day by walking around and greeting all my staff."
- "I'm dedicated to this profession. In fact, I started asking for books on architecture when I was in the second grade."
- "I get results. I was honored to earn President's Club–level sales in each of my eight years at IBM."

Being specific often means including meaningful and measurable results, making your points using hard numbers. You're not fully prepared for an interview without spelling out the results you've achieved. Remember the Job Match Matrix? Think of all the metrics you could add: How many years? How many people? How much sold? How many projects? Include growth percentages, reductions in waste, productivity efficiencies, time to market, courses taught. This data should be top of mind in case you need it to prove an answer about your skills.

An executive was referred to me by several sources. "Calvin is top-notch!" they all said. When I met with him, he remarked that he had been participating in interviews lately because his organization was relocating. "I keep getting face-to-face interviews," Calvin told me, "but I've never been selected as a finalist."

When I interviewed him myself several weeks later for one of my searches, the reason he was falling short became obvious. When I asked specific questions about skills, I got broad generalizations for answers. I remember asking Calvin, "How much money did you raise in the annual campaign that year?" (My client's campaign hovered around $3 million annually, and my client wanted someone who had raised at least $1 million in a year.) "Oh, we had great success," Calvin said. "We brought in some new communication methods, which was really exciting."

After the interview, I talked with Calvin about using meaningful and measurable results to make the case for his skills. For example, when answering the question about the amount raised in the annual campaign, Calvin could have said, "This year's campaign raised $1.2 million, $100,000 over goal. We attributed the success to communication approaches that targeted new audiences." I encouraged Calvin to use this meaningful result as the core answer to a skill question. He could always fill out the context with other details, but those numbers were essential. Calvin shored up his use of meaningful and measurable results, and soon after that conversation, he obtained a new position.

➜ TIP 8: TELL REAL STORIES FROM YOUR WORK HISTORY

I revealed my true feelings some pages back when I said I cringe at canned stories. Don't let that caution, however, scare you away from sharing real-life illustrations. The most persuasive case you can make for your candidacy often comes from drawing your listeners into real work events, illustrating your points by drawing word pictures of actual situations. Maybe a particular story includes a meaningful and measurable result. Even stories without obvious metrics are good; they humanize you and show what makes you tick. Share an authentic moment, and your likeability quotient almost certainly goes up.

As beneficial as examples are in an interview, be careful not to get too wordy. I've watched many terrific examples turn into trips down memory lane. I once saw a director-level candidate give a 19-minute example. Even though the story matched the question, the whole room drowned in a sea of excessive verbiage.

Interviewing often involves an impromptu filling out of the details of the "for instances" I mentioned earlier. For example, you might talk about points like these:

- What was going on at the start of your story? Was your organization suffering a major pain point? Facing an opportunity for positive growth? What was your team thinking and feeling?

- What did you personally do about the situation? What was your exact role? How did you motivate and mobilize others to act? How did they respond to your leadership?

- What was the outcome? What happened? Once the situation was resolved, what did you learn? How did you grow? Could you have done something even better? How? Have you furthered your skills since then?

The details you choose to include in your story should speak to the question at hand. Where do you go from there? It's your real story, right? It impacted you and others, correct? For just a moment, transport yourself back to that setting and tell your story concisely but from the heart.

Caution: Don't let nostalgia for an important career event send you off on tangents. Don't expand your story with details that don't add to your answer. Keep your examples brief and positive. If your listeners want more details, they can ask follow-up questions.

Current or recent examples are usually best at making your point. First, the interviewing organization probably placed more emphasis on your recent experiences when reviewing your credentials and deciding to call you in. Your interviewers will likely be most interested in having you flesh out those roles. Second, more recent experiences might well be more relevant and meaningful.

I began my career in training and development at IBM. It was a terrific experience, and I learned much that has informed my career in the decades since. If an interviewer asked me about using media in training presentations now, however, I'd shy away from pulling up that job as an illustration. In those years, we presented from overhead projectors, mostly. We plunked away on IBM Selectric typewriters to prep training materials. If we wanted graphics to adorn our handouts, we drew them by hand on the page!

Even if a good illustration could answer several interview questions, don't reuse a situation. Let's say that three years ago you assembled a team of product engineers to focus on high-value clients. Your team brought in more new busi- ness than any other product group in the company's history. Congratulations! Your example could answer a question like "What's the most effective team you've ever worked with?" Or "What accomplishment are you most proud of?" Or "What's been your most difficult professional challenge?" Even if your story is a doozy, resist the urge to retell it for multiple questions. Better to highlight other successful projects and achievements from diverse parts of your career.

Here's the power of authentic story: A single, well-told, real-life example will drive your point home far more effectively than a thousand quotations from popular business books. After all, interview questions are directed toward you, so your answers should be about *you*. Be ready to talk specifically about the real-life results of your leadership approach just as you gather metrics from your process improvements or technical insights.

It's a good bet that other candidates will roll out phrases from the latest business best-sellers. Be the candidate who doesn't parrot well-known platitudes. Those answers, however well-delivered, always come across hollow and thin.

➜ TIP 9: BE POINTED WITH ANY PERSONAL STORIES

Stories from your personal life have a somewhat limited role in an interview. Funny tales that guarantee a laugh are usually best at a bar. They *might* be a good use of your interview time but only if they strongly make the point at hand.

I watched personal stories get in the way of an interview of one of the most talented executives I've ever represented. Wayne made more than $2 million each year as chief financial officer at a Fortune 500 company. He was interviewing to become the CEO of a national nonprofit where his skills, background, and education were a good match.

When I reviewed Wayne's background with the interviewing board of directors, they were, not surprisingly, highly interested in his candidacy. He'd won numerous awards, was clearly tops in his field, and they wanted to meet him in person. The board raised just one tiny red flag—that Wayne had moved around a bit in his career. Two jobs in particular stood out, with each lasting less than two years. Wayne had given compelling explanations for those situations when I interviewed him (in one case the company was sold, and in the other he took a different job to be closer to an ill family member). I suggested that the board query Wayne on this point in the interview. We drafted a question requesting a brief career synopsis.

Before the interview, I spoke with Wayne, suggesting he keep his career summary short and on point. If the interviewers needed more content, they would ask follow-up questions. Wayne agreed to give a compact career history without extra trimmings.

The interview day arrived and the meeting hummed along, with Wayne at his impressive best. Then came time to ask Wayne for a brief summary of a few parts of his career.

And off to the races Wayne went. Although the question deliberately didn't ask for early history, Wayne told about his growing up years. And he told how he had selected his college. Activities he'd enjoyed as a fraternity man. The serendipitous way he'd gotten his first job. His funny boss. Interesting conferences. Geographical moves. Detailed examples of how things went "in the old days."

The whole thing took 25 minutes. That's right, 25 minutes! Wayne had entered the interview as the top candidate but left having raised significant questions about his ability to communicate and manage time, important parts of the job he was seeking.

The bottom line is this: In an interview, personal stories from your early history have value only to the extent that they closely answer an interview question.

➔ TIP 10: HONOR TIME

Years ago I bought a book about public speaking. A little book, barely more than a pamphlet, that taught me things I remember 30 years later. Top tip? The first message you should send an audience is that you'll honor their time. Think about it. When you're a part of an audience, you expect the speaker to honor time constraints. If the speaker appears unaware or disrespectful of the limits, how do you feel? That little book suggests that speakers who go over the time budget are telling the audience, "what I want to say is more important than anything else that you have to do at this point."

Excessively lengthy answers, tangents, and continuing to talk past the scheduled time say the same thing to a hiring executive that a verbose speaker communicates to a weary audience: "My long answer is more important than your deadline." Definitely *not* a message that makes a positive impression.

Maybe you can get away with an occasional expanded answer with an acknowledgement about its length ("I realize that answer was lengthy; thanks for allowing me to provide the extra detail."), but what the interviewer immediately envisions is you sitting in a meeting with a key client, needing to make a brief point before time is up, yet yammering on and on and on. The interviewer might further picture you in a regularly scheduled 20-minute product-update session and see you telling minimally relevant tales that take the meeting off-track and overtime.

> **Successful executives exhibit outstanding self-management in a variety of contexts, including skillful time management.** You probably do this naturally in the workplace. It's absolutely imperative that you demonstrate the same ability in an interview. I cannot stress this enough.

Remember that the more you talk, the less believable you are. It makes the listener wonder, *What's this person trying to cover up under all those meaningless words?* You don't need to overexplain or repeat yourself to make your point. If you really have more to say, ask if you can expand up your answer or offer another example. Let the interviewer opt in or out of hearing more. If the interviewers say they got it, well, they've got it. Don't go on further.

TIP 11:
HONOR *EVERYONE* YOU MEET

A friend of mine works in an office that has a steady stream of executives flowing in and out. Who do you suppose she and her coworkers ask when they want to get an accurate read on who one of those executives really is? The administrative associate at the front desk.

How do you treat people in the interview process who aren't part of the decision-making team? Remember that all interactions during the process are fair game. Be gracious and positive to all you encounter. Think of each as a potential new colleague. My friend has a simple hiring rule: Treat an associate badly, and you'll never work at the company.

It's up to you, the candidate, to treat every member of the interviewing organization with dignity and kindness. Be a person any of them would love to work with every day.

By the way, interviewers are people, too. Giving them positive feedback goes a long way toward lowering everyone's stress and creating connections. If a question is particularly insightful or unique or relevant, say so. "I've never been asked that question before, and it's a good one." Or, "Hmmm, that's a valuable point."

When you do something well, you like positive feedback. Right? Good comments have a noticeable effect on a candidate. Comments like "That's a good answer" or "Great overview, very relevant, thanks" cause a candidate to sit up straight and gain confidence. That upbeat interaction goes both ways, and can work wonders in warming up an interview.

➔ TIP 12: REMEMBER THAT ACTIONS SPEAK LOUDER THAN WORDS

Never is this sentiment more relevant than in an interview! As an interviewee, keep this constantly in mind. Let me offer a few examples:

In one case, a candidate answered a question about her work style as "prepared," citing the planning she undertakes to ensure she's never blindsided in meetings. She went on about how she always reviews pertinent information ahead of time. But when this candidate got her chance to ask the interviewer anything she wished, she rolled out simple questions that could be answered with a half-minute visit to the home page of the company website!

The hiring executive commented later that the interviewing team was concerned about the candidate's ability to take charge of purchasing million-dollar machines. The hiring executive said she "couldn't put her finger on it" (I could!), but she had real doubts the candidate could manage rigorous, detailed information gathering. A lack of the preparedness she touted ended that candidate's hopes for a job she really wanted.

In another situation, a candidate for a director of human resources position described herself as "a people person." She said, "As a matter of fact, that's my top strength—my ability to connect with others!" Yet when one of her answers prompted an interviewer to request clarification, she responded brusquely. "I think my answer was clear enough—but, oh well…" When asked how she coaches lower performers, her reply began with this: "Well, you know how those types are; sometimes they just don't get it!"

Result? The candidate's strong background wasn't enough to compensate for her poor showing of the people skills she said she possessed.

A mismatch between your words and your actions never escapes notice, even if it's a vague feeling of "I can't quite put my finger on it. Something just doesn't seem to fit."

CHAPTER 21

THE GROUP INTERVIEW

"WHAT ABOUT OUR COMPANY INTERESTS YOU?"

Petra glanced around the conference table. She was glad for the chance to meet the folks who would be her peers at Byhram Nash, but she knew a group interview can be challenging.

The question came from Murray Wallace, the HR leader she'd spoken with earlier. *Seems like a sharp, capable guy*, she thought. Others around the table were Rian Lee, head of manufacturing; Corey Washington, head of finance; and Bea Bianco, leader of quality and supply chain functions. On the phone was Ann Lennin, head of engineering, who was on assignment in another city.

Petra nodded. "That's a good question, Murray. Right now I'm not unhappy. I'm in a fine position in my current company. But there are several things that appeal to me about Byhram Nash and this role in particular. First . . ."

This wasn't an unexpected question, and Petra was ready. She had a handful of thoughts to share with the group. She knew her best approach would ***not*** be flattery or excessively flowery descriptions. She kept her response positive yet honest, balancing aspects of the role that fit her interests and career path with what she could bring to Byhram Nash.

By the end of her answer, the group nodded and seemed satisfied.

Next, Ann asked Petra if she had a noncompete agreement that could affect her ability to work with certain customers. "Again, a good question," Petra smiled. "No, not with my current company."

Although Petra was in the role of interviewee, as time went on, the interview felt like a conversation. There were follow-up questions, a couple of tangents, and a bit of humor. Petra knew that everyone present was assessing not just her skills in the sales and marketing function but her fit as a potential member of their team.

There was a short pause. Rian spoke up. "I've heard there were hiccups with your company's last product launch. Could you talk about that?" A tough question. One Petra didn't look forward to discussing. Mistakes had occurred. A couple of errors were Petra's, and she was ready to own them and explain how she learned from them. Several coworkers had also made mistakes, and she wasn't sure how to address those. Petra absolutely didn't want to mention anyone by name or title. This is a small world, and folks know each other.

"Thanks, Rian." She paused. "Ultimately the product was launched, and we're now off and running. But there were, as you mentioned, some hiccups—two are relevant for my role. One was that we got to market later than expected. The other was that we didn't contact some of our key clients right away. I own those errors. Let me share a bit about that situation and what we learned." Even though Rian had posed the question, Petra deliberately answered the full group, making eye contact and connecting with each. She knew the peril of getting into a two-person "closed loop" interaction when a difficult topic emerged. At the end of her answer, she again looked around the table, a simple visual check-in with each person that she'd learned to implement in her everyday group meetings.

When the interview questions were completed, Murray asked Petra if she'd brought any questions for them. She had, indeed. The big one. "Yes. What's Deonne really like to work for?" After a chuckle, the group answered. Petra listened intently. She followed up. After another question about the senior leadership team's planning process, she wrapped up.

As Petra said good-bye to the leadership team, she thanked each person by name, making a comment specific to that person's part of the interview. As she walked out the door, she turned. Looking back over her shoulder, she said, "Thank you all! I hope we have another opportunity to talk soon!"

CHAPTER 22

GROUP INTERVIEW HOW-TO

TO BE AN EXECUTIVE OFTEN MEANS YOU SPEND YOUR LIFE IN MEETINGS. You're likely highly skilled at leading them. You've probably had many turns in the hot seat, surrounded by curious, hopeful, and even hostile faces. A job interview brings a unique twist on those experiences. Most significantly, the people across the table aren't your usual crowd—your team, your peers, your superiors, or other stakeholders who normally fill the room. It's crucial in an interview setting to make a quick and personable connection with everyone present.

At some point in your interview process, it's likely you'll encounter more than one face on the other side of a conference table. You might be seated with a couple of people, or you might find yourself among what feels like a crowd (a mob?). Whatever the size of the group in "group interview," **consider these tips:**

LEARN AND REMEMBER. A senior manager arrived to interview with a fairly sizeable board of directors, perhaps 15 people. Prior to the meeting, she'd looked up each individual online. As she entered the boardroom, she shook hands with each board member and called each by name. She made a comment to each related to the person's background or other distinguishing fact. Impressive!

Another CEO candidate, in contrast, arrived to meet an interviewing board of eight. "Don't worry," he said as he shook hands and was introduced to each. "I won't remember your names anyway!"

Your proficiency with names and personal details is a small yet precious indicator of how you treat other important information. What conclusions would you have drawn about the candidates from the above interactions? What could you surmise about how such a leader would treat employees or customers? Or how well he or she would capture and recall important data?

ANSWER TO THE GROUP. This advice comes from my short-lived but much-beloved career as a public-speaking coach: ***Remember that a group is a group.*** A group is an entity. A collective. A question from one person is a question from all. This is especially true if the question is difficult or challenging. Treat a question from one member as a question from the entire group. Listen carefully to the person asking the question. When you answer, address everyone, not just the individual who raised the question. Work very hard at this, as it makes a huge difference.

INJECT HUMOR. Group interviews have a propensity to be dry or staid. Multiple people jockey with multiple questions, causing a greater concern for logistics (not stumbling over each other) and time (watching the clock). A recent candidate was asked a question about how he would assess an organization. Within his answer, he mentioned that he would spend a lot of time listening. "Not that you can tell that about me right now," he added, "since I've been talking 80 percent of the time so far!" It was funny. The group laughter broke the tension of the tight structure. If the moment feels right, it's okay to add a light comment. Sometimes groups can use it.

ASK QUESTIONS RELEVANT TO *THE GROUP*. Think about the unique questions you might ask of the specific group you're meeting with. If it's a team of senior leaders who would be your peers, what might you want to hear from them? Good questions could include asking about how they work together: "What planning process do you use?" "How often does this group interact?" "How would you describe the culture within the senior management team?" "What is the boss really like to work for?" If the interview brings together a team that would report directly to you, consider asking their input on what they want in a new boss. Or ask, "What current projects are the most exciting for you? The most challenging?" or "What are your hopes for the coming year?"

I've already hinted at this final thought: Keep in mind the perspective of each person in the room. Board members might be focused on assessing your strategic abilities or even your suitability for future promotions in the organization. People who would work for you wonder how you manage in real life. Peers may be trying to picture how you would function as a member of their team, that is, as a fellow participant in their Monday Morning Staff Meetings!

CHAPTER 23

A DOZEN COMMON INTERVIEW QUESTIONS

Of all the topics that can surface in an interview, a handful are most likely to come up in one form or another. I'd like to present several common questions and talk about the best ways to handle them. For each example question, I'll share these explanations:

FIRST INSTINCT: typical assumptions about the "right" answer or how you might be tempted to respond

UNINTENDED RESULT: how a misguided answer can sound to an interviewer

DO THIS INSTEAD: the best approach to tackling each common question

➔ QUESTION 1: WHAT ARE YOU LOOKING FOR IN YOUR NEXT JOB?

This question always appears on my list. It's more broadly phrased than another question I often ask, "Why are you interested in this job?" This question's broader wording gives me a better sense of a candidate's overall perspective.

FIRST INSTINCT: You might feel tempted to focus solely on what *you* want from your next role. For example, a recent CFO candidate replied, "I'm seeking a collaborative work environment where I can continue to learn and grow." Anything else? "I'd like a strong focus on professional development, such as attending industry conferences or perhaps working with an executive coach." He also threw in that "something closer to home would be nice."

UNINTENDED RESULT: That answer will likely come across as self-serving. After all, it's one-sided—your side!

Keep in mind that a prospective employer is purchasing your services. Before you launch into what *you* need and want, make sure you've understood and addressed what that *employer* needs. Here's a rule of thumb: The earlier it is in the interview process, the more likely questions will focus on what you can contribute—and so should your answers. Usually, the best time for raising your own concerns is later in the process. If what you're looking for hasn't been satisfactorily heard or addressed, you can certainly bring it up.

Interviews open the door for you to share 1) what you can contribute to the company and 2) what it can provide for you. Balance and timing are crucial.

DO THIS INSTEAD: Your answer should come from a place of understanding that a dream job consists of multiple factors:

- Title
- Work content
- Responsibility/Scope
- Organizational culture
- Characteristics of a work group or department
- Qualities of your manager or board
- Opportunities to travel (or not have to travel)
- Compensation and benefits
- Chances to learn and grow

As you answer the question "What are you looking for in your next job?" recall what led you to consider a job change in the first place—the things you need and want in your next job. That likely includes both quantitative and qualitative factors.

Quantitative factors are points like salary, scope of job, title, and travel requirements.

Qualitative factors include work culture, organizational mission, culture, colleagues, things to build or fix, and development opportunities.

Most job seekers value qualitative factors over quantitative factors, but consider both. For each key factor, determine what to you represents a deal breaker. By settling this ahead of time, your responses won't be colored by a specific role. You also won't find yourself caught up in the excitement of an interview process, overselling yourself for a job that isn't a great match. Use your list of needs, wants, and deal breakers to guide your inquiries.

A recent candidate for VP of government affairs said, "After five years at my current organization, I feel ready for the challenge of the VP position and the chance to practice in a larger and somewhat more complex environment. Also, I've become a regional expert on the regulations in this sector and would love the chance to apply that knowledge in a growing organization where that thought leadership could have real value." Do you hear the balance between organizational and personal needs?

➔ QUESTION 2: TELL ME ABOUT YOURSELF

FIRST INSTINCT: This question might prompt you to spill every last detail about yourself. After all, you're a very inter- esting person. You might be tempted to weave a tale of your idyllic upbringing on the farm, your crazy college days, the story behind each bullet of your résumé, and a laundry list of your many accomplishments.

UNINTENDED RESULT: That approach raises red flags all around. A rambling answer signals to an employer that you can't take a load of information and selectively highlight the most pertinent. It could suggest a time-management issue. By undercutting the give-and-take of an interview, it raises concerns about your ability to understand context and perceive social cues. It could also come across as "I think that everything about me is amazing."

A long summary statement shortchanges you. It risks your audience tuning you out. It leaves no room for further probing. And if you run out of time and never get to later questions, you miss the meatiest parts of the discussion.

The vice president of a large nonprofit organization opened an interview for a director of operations with "Could you tell me a bit about yourself and your background?" He maybe even added "in two or three minutes." Well, the candidate took off. After seven minutes, the VP raised his hand, visually suggesting he'd like to retake the floor. At 18 minutes, the VP tried to break in verbally. The candidate kept right on going. Eventually, the candidate wrapped up his exceptionally long answer. Nearly a third of the allotted interview time had vanished, with only one question down.

The vice president was gracious. "Wow," he said when he was finally allowed to speak. "That answer sure covered a lot of ground!" The candidate grinned and nodded, thinking the vice president was paying him a compliment! In the end, the candidate wasn't selected to move on to the next hiring round.

DO THIS INSTEAD: This question often opens the interview. It elicits context for everything that follows, inviting you to paint an overall picture of yourself while leaving room for other questions and answers to fill in the details. You've answered well if the interviewer gets a handle on your distinct areas of expertise and what sets you apart.

Answer positively but modestly. Starting with a few brief statements, perhaps mentioning a key influencer or two from your early days, is a good backdrop, especially if that information explains your passion for your field. Next, a high-level overview of your work experience is useful. A job-by-job history isn't appropriate. A broader and more thematic answer, hitting major stages or turning points, is better. Finally, you might mention civic or community boards or activities you participate in, especially if they add valuable experience or offer insight into your personality and interests.

You should be able to filter and share the most important elements of your work life in *two or three minutes*. Just recognize that you shouldn't memorize even this brief overview. The points worth including can change significantly from one setting to another!

➔ QUESTION 3: WHY ARE YOU LOOKING TO LEAVE YOUR CURRENT ORGANIZATION?

FIRST INSTINCT: This question might sound like a prime opportunity to share that your boss is ineffective, and that you're vastly overworked and underappreciated. Or maybe it's a chance to dispute the raw deal when you were passed over for a promotion that was given to someone less qualified. If a litany of irritants illustrates that your current situation is less than perfect, you might be tempted to list them all.

UNINTENDED RESULT: Even if all of the above is true, you'll only sound bitter and unhappy. *That's okay*, you think. *I am bitter and unhappy!* But here's the thing. You're only one side of the equation. Your interviewer has no way of knowing if your current setting is in fact a living nightmare *or* whether you're just prone to complaining and can be expected to do more of the same at a new organization.

For interviewers, this is an "If I had a dollar for every complaint I've heard . . ." kind of moment. The charges might be absolutely legitimate, and yet complaining never pays off. I frequently hear hiring executives, following interviews where the candidate launched into criticisms of their current or former employer, say, "That's strange. I know plenty of people who work in that company, and they all like it!" Worse, you might be attacking someone the interviewer knows!

DO THIS INSTEAD: You're always better off suggesting that the new job is a move *toward* something rather than *away* from something. The interviewing company will always prefer a candidate with thoughtful and positive reasons for showing interest in the organization and role. No one likes being your getaway plan from your current untenable situation. Consider these responses, for example:

QUESTION: Why do you want to leave?

ANSWER: "I'm really unhappy with the blatant favoritism shown to another member of our team. The VP does nothing to stop my boss from giving the best assignments to her happy hour buddy. It leaves me handling the leftovers—a bunch of difficult, underperforming clients. It's an impossible situation!"

BETTER ANSWER: "There are many things I like about my current situation, including the chance to work on complex client projects. But I like the (insert "product line," "increased responsibilities," "larger portfolio," or other attractive features) in this new opportunity. I'm also attracted to what I've seen so far of the culture. It all makes me interested in exploring more."

➔ QUESTION 4: HOW WELL DO YOU THINK YOU FIT THIS POSITION?

FIRST INSTINCT: You might be tempted to say you're a perfect fit for a role. Indeed, you might feel you have it all—that you're the best of the breed.

UNINTENDED RESULT: The "I'm perfect for this job" answer never plays well. It could come across at a minimum as ill-informed, but, more likely, as wildly oblivious. And that's on a good day. Overselling is never attractive.

Particularly at a first or second interview, how can you possibly know whether you're a "perfect" fit? It's like saying you're a perfect marriage match with someone you just met! Granted, you may see areas of commonality. You might quickly sense you would get along well. Time might even reveal you're 100 percent correct. But you're so early in the game that even if you *are* the ideal fit, you lack the information to make that pronouncement. Hence, you come across as careless and ignorant.

Take a look at the factors needed to determine whether a candidate is the "perfect" fit:

- The organization's culture, as a whole and in a specific business group
- The hiring executive's management style
- Members of the team you'd join (and how you would complement the team)
- Type of staff you'd manage (and what the staff currently needs in a leader)

- Goals and objectives for the position
- Challenges of the position (usually not identified in the job description)
- Skeletons in the closet (every job has several)
- Office politics (every organization has them)
- New initiatives and strategies (including those not yet announced)
- Upcoming personnel changes (including those not yet public)
- And many, many others!

Think about it. Can you really be certain you're "a perfect fit" for this job?

DO THIS INSTEAD: Start with the realization that no individual is perfect for anything, including any particular job. Realize, also, that if you're using the job description as a guide to "perfect," that job descriptions can't possibly cover everything. Moreover, what an employer truly needs in a candidate can shift throughout the process.

To be safe, don't use the word "perfect" at any stage of the interview process. With the word "perfect" out of your vocabulary, focus on answering thoughtfully. The underlying point of this question is all about discernment.

Your best answer might begin with an overview of the areas where you believe your strengths match up well with what you know about the job. Then summarize the areas that you think may not fit as well. Be absolutely honest. Really. You probably consider yourself a pretty darn good fit for a number of reasons, but there might still be areas to explore.

A vice president of international sourcing gave a good answer. "From what I know so far," he said, "I think there's a good fit. I've run departments of about the same size and I've sourced from many of the same vendors and locations. That said, I'm eager to learn more. Every organization is different, and I'm sure that's reflected in different approaches in the sourcing function."

➜ QUESTION 5: WHAT AREYOUR AREAS FOR DEVELOPMENT? (What are your weaknesses?)

FIRST INSTINCT: You might be tempted to follow the old adage that says, "Turn a negative into a positive." Goodness knows there are enough books about job interviewing that push this advice. You could, for example, say, "I'm a workaholic. I put in so many hours at the office that I don't have any hobbies. That's my area for development." Or you could say, "I'm a perfectionist. I double- and triple-check my work. My extra effort sets an impossibly high standard for others and makes them feel bad. I really need to work on lowering my impossibly high standards for myself."

UNINTENDED RESULT: You come across like an executive using dated interviewing advice that even high schoolers know not to use. Maybe you could fake your way through the hiring process, hoping none of the interviewers has ever heard this ruse (not likely).

These made-up "weaknesses" suggest two things to me, neither of which is good. First, your real deficiency is too scary to share, so you decided to make something up (which comes across as dishonest). Second, you don't know or can't articulate your deficiencies (which comes across as possessing poor self-awareness).

We *all* have deficiencies. Virtually all managers and executives have had opportunities to identify their strengths and weaknesses through training, coaching, performance appraisals, psychological assessments, or leadership-development activities. Heck, if you've never experienced this kind of feedback, just ask your significant other, friends, or loved ones to kindly fill you in. I'm sure they'll oblige!

It's important you come into the interview process prepared to answer this question. You could review past performance-review forms, scan past management assessments, ask for fresh 360-degree feedback, or go online and take a leadership assessment right now.

DO THIS INSTEAD: You shouldn't be surprised I'm advising you to answer with 100 percent honesty. Whatever you need to work on, say it.

One of my own weaknesses is that at times I can be thin-skinned. I don't like to hear negative feedback, and I don't always process criticism well. I know this about myself. I don't run from it. I really don't have any reason to hide this truth when I'm asked point-blank about my deficiencies. I also don't like conflict. I avoid it. If I were interviewing at a company rife with conflict, where things get personal and people use disagreement to advance their agendas, I'd want to know that. I would hope my honest answer would lead to my *not* being selected for that job!

I once worked at a small consulting company. The owner, either a genius or a sadist, made me do an exercise I still remember 30 years later. Because we trained people in public speaking, we spent most of our days in front of audiences. The owner, a renowned trainer, told me to pull out a blank sheet of paper. She asked me to envision myself in front of a group. Then she told me to list anything negative an audience member might see in me.

I can't remember exactly what I wrote, but the list likely contained a self-assessment of physical characteristics I was lacking (Marcia is too scrawny, Marcia has a biggish nose, Marcia's voice can be nasally). I probably included behaviors I felt needed fixing (Marcia can be wishy-washy, Marcia doesn't give tough critiques, and so on).

I had bared my soul. I probably smiled at my honest self-critique. I brought my list to the owner. She looked it over and pronounced it "average." She told me to add more self-critical comments.

My second round must have pleased her, because she told me the assignment was done. "There," she said. "Now you won't have to be afraid of negative feedback. You already know most of what the audience could say. It's on your list!"

Am I suggesting you make your own list? Maybe. Maybe. What I'm suggesting for sure is that you know yourself well enough to answer the weakness question with a healthy self-awareness and the confidence that comes from knowing that all individuals have faults to discuss. You are, after all, interviewing for this job as a complete package.

Hiding your weaknesses falls short of every one of the universal attributes employers desire. As a reminder, from Chapter 5, any organization worth working for seeks employees who display the universal attributes of:

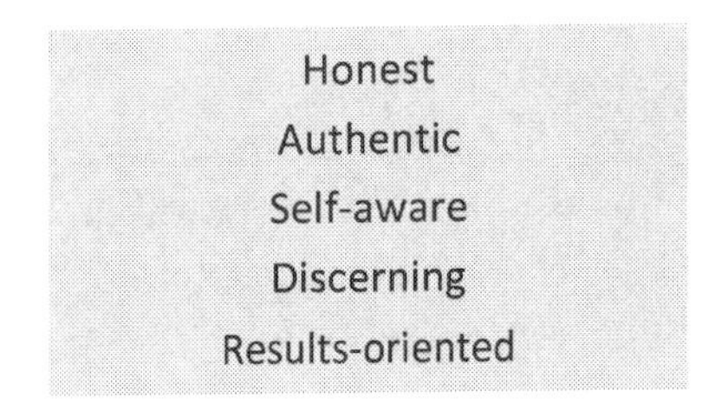

The key to a good answer about your deficiencies is 1) having enough self- awareness to identify your weakness, and 2) understanding how a particular weakness could impact your ability to succeed in a job. This awareness also includes knowing what you need to do, or have already done, to ensure this weakness isn't an ongoing hurdle.

Knowledge of a weakness is one thing. Everyone has them. Not doing anything to compensate for a weakness or minimize its impact is worse than the weakness itself.

I once interviewed a vice president of research analytics. When I asked about her weaknesses, she looked me straight in the eye and said, "Doughnuts!" I gave her points for humor, but the answer didn't tell me anything about how her weakness might do damage to her work.

By this point in your career, not only do you probably know a few of your less desirable characteristics, but you've also had opportunities to work on them. You've maybe had access to leadership coaching, or personal-development training, to bolster an area. Don't hesitate to add this information in your answer. In fact, I encourage you to do so. Here's a great formula for answering this question:

- Development area
- How you addressed it
- Improvements you've noticed
- Continuing efforts to address the issue (optional)

It's not wrong to state that you're still involved in professional development related to your improvement area. I worked with an executive who prided herself on her efficiency, including her ability to juggle many priorities. Other leaders looked to her as the "get it done" person. In her pursuit of efficiency, however, she stepped on a lot of toes. She developed a reputation of being prickly and unapproachable. When she received feedback about her style, she took it seriously and committed to working on relationship building. She slowed down and learned how to put relationships before tasks. She did more asking and less telling. She softened her emails, even using a softer font. She knew she needed an ongoing effort toward her development goal to avoid reverting to her old style. When she was open about her learning in an interview, she demonstrated her receptivity to feedback and ability to change.

➔ QUESTION 6: WHAT IS YOUR LEADERSHIP STYLE?

FIRST INSTINCT: I've pointed out how easy it is to wax philosophical about leadership. It's tempting to use trendy leadership words from current books, blogs, and other pop media. After all, wouldn't doing so make you look well-read?

You could say, for example, "Leadership is so important. Businesses rise and fall on the leadership skills within their organizations. Collaboration is at the heart of leadership. Leaders are only as good as the connection they have with staff." And so on.

UNINTENDED RESULT: Yawn. A philosophical-type answer comes across as generic. Impersonal. One-size-fits-no-one. Notice that the question asks about *your* leadership style, not the impressions of some author or guru, no matter how impressive that person is. The question aims to open a dialogue about your own style and how well that style fits the hiring organization.

DO THIS INSTEAD: **Answer a question about *you* by talking about *you*. Make the answer as personal as you can, using themes from real-life input.** If you've participated in a

360-degree review, talk about the results of that process. What did your staff identify as strengths of your leadership style? What examples did they cite? How have you capitalized on these strengths? Where did your assessors say you need development? How have you worked to overcome those gaps? If you haven't participated in a 360, recall past performance reviews. What did your boss say about your leadership skills? What have others said informally about how you lead?

Does any of that feedback help you formulate an answer to the question? I'm guessing much of it does. **Remember, a specific example better allows the interviewer to picture what your leadership looks like in practice.**

A candidate for president of an economic-development organization answered this question well. She explained that she had had the great opportunity to attend a two-week leadership development program at the renowned Center for Creative Leadership. In preparation for the program, several members of her staff received a questionnaire about her leadership. At the center, an industrial psychologist reviewed the staff input with her.

As the candidate shared this information with me, she was precise about the feedback she had received as well as what she had learned about herself. She recounted the exact language her staff had used to describe her leadership style. She offered to give me a copy of the results. Thoroughly impressive.

➔ QUESTION 7: TELL ME ABOUT YOUR EXPERIENCE WITH ______ (something that's a distinct strength)

FIRST INSTINCT: This question feels like a softball right in your wheelhouse. Home run! You're asked about an area you claim as a strength. Fantastic! You might snap to this chance to toot your own horn. You might also be tempted to dress up a related area that isn't as solid. Who will ever know?

UNINTENDED RESULT: Caution: Are you sure you're sharing an actual strength area? For example, suppose you have 15 years of leadership experience in product quality. If the question asks about your quality-systems background, you might feel you can outperform anyone. But your specific experience is exclusively in lean manufacturing. Are you sure the organization uses lean and not some other methodology?

Or let's say you inherited a mediocre program and built your reputation by steadily improving it over the years. What if the interviewing company needs someone to start a program from scratch? What if it prefers consultants to run the program with only light oversight from inside?

Don't forget that you're likely competing against other candidates. You might have 15 years of product-quality experience, but what if all the other candidates have 30?

DO THIS INSTEAD: Normally, this question looks for technical, operational, or content skills. Candidates who focus only on interpersonal or management skills in their answers miss an opportunity to frame up their hard-skill background in light of the available position. If in doubt, you can ask, "Would you like me to focus more on my technical or operational background—or more on my people skills?" Or you can address your background for most of the answer and finish with a short statement about interpersonal skills.

The best answers to this question have two parts. First, include your own brief assessment of your experience. Second, mention how others have assessed your experience. While your own opinion about your greatness certainly matters, the opinions of others about your top attributes have even more value.

I observed a general manager candidate answer this question exceptionally well in an interview for a large manufacturing firm with more than 20 production facilities worldwide. The interviewer asked about the candidate's experience with international operations and global product lines. The candidate answered by saying, "I think my international work is a distinct strength, because it includes two expatriate assignments, one in the European Union and one in Hong Kong. The latter gave me broad responsibilities for six Asian facilities. Second, from my early years with your top competitor, I have a fairly deep understanding of your product line. With a brief onboarding, I think I could hit the ground running from a product standpoint. I should add that over the years others have complimented me on my ability to manage complex international-finance issues. I know my way around a financial statement, at least according to my peers. When I left my last job, my boss and the team gave me a pair of green sunglasses as a going-away gift! Over the years, that comment has been repeated on almost all of my performance reviews."

Be careful of the trap to oversell a skill set you think is attractive to the employer but isn't *really* a strength of yours. Executives who sell a skill set that's truly not in their sweet spot sometimes land the job but struggle to succeed. Getting the job is only the first step. Doing the job is a looong second step!

➔ QUESTION 8: TELL ME ABOUT YOUR EXPERIENCE WITH ______ (something that's a weakness)

FIRST INSTINCT: Uh oh. This is difficult. While it resembles Question 5, there's a subtle difference. It's getting at a specific job requirement. The usual weakness question is more generic and you can respond about any workplace skill or behavior.

As you attempt to answer this question, keep in mind one of my original premises: You're at the interview because you're seen as a strong candidate. You're probably quite able to do the job. Don't let a question about one job requirement take you off your course of honesty and integrity.

The problem is this: You're being asked about an area obviously vital to the job where you happen to not excel. Unless you duck and maneuver and distract the interviewer to avoid the question, you'll have to respond. But how? Your might break a sweat as your mind scrambles for an answer, something that's genuine yet doesn't derail your chances. You could cover up your weakness by exaggerating whatever level of skill you do have. Or you could minimize the importance of the skill to succeeding at the job. Or you could obfuscate. These tactics are among the most common interviewing mistakes I see.

Let's say you're interviewing for a role that includes overseeing two plants in Mexico. You'll need to travel there frequently and work on issues with Spanish-speaking staff and vendors. Twenty-two years ago, you had a year of high school Spanish. Except for retaining a few words, however, it's gone.

So what will you do if the question is "How well do you speak Spanish?"

You could choose to cover up your lack of skill, saying

you speak "well enough" or "pretty good," or stating that "yes, that would be fine."

You could choose to obfuscate, asserting something not entirely wrong but not altogether accurate, such as, "Yes, I have had previous training in Spanish and I very much enjoyed it."

You could choose to minimize the importance of the skill, even negating the need for language ability, saying, "Nowadays most people speak English, so Spanish isn't that important for these types of jobs." Or "Translators are available everywhere, so I'd just hire one of them."

From my perch in the back of the interview room, I've heard these responses too many times to count, and I cringe every time. I watch the interviewer's face flash an expression of wonderment at how the candidate can feel justified in weighing in on or even criticizing a legitimate job requirement.

UNINTENDED RESULT: Interviewers almost always see through these misguided answers. Can you imagine an interviewer responding to your "stretch" answers in Spanish? And expecting your response in Spanish? Anything even slightly less than the full truth sends the message that you're dishonest, and an answer that appears to stretch your background or skills can call into question all your other answers.

DO THIS INSTEAD: Remember my basic premise. You've been invited to interview by people who've studied your résumé. They may already sense your strengths and weaknesses. Don't, under any circumstances, fudge or overstate your abilities. You'll be bounced from consideration faster than you can say, "I'm good at everything!"

Consider this answer: "Wow, that's exciting. While I do have experience overseeing plants outside of the U.S., I have to admit my Spanish would be considered 'traveler Spanish' at best. I've seen advertisements for executive language-immersion courses that are as brief as two on-site weeks. I'd be happy to take such a course at the company's direction, in order to get my language skills up to speed."

Another possibility would be to first clarify the question. You could ask, "I see Spanish is a preferred requirement of the job. Tell me exactly the level of Spanish needed to be effective in this role. Is it daily conversational? Does it also require reading or writing in Spanish?" This clarifying information can help you respond. "Recognizing the importance of being able to clearly communicate across the entire organization," you could say, "I would set a priority of taking an immersion class in conversational and business Spanish within the first 90 days."

I interviewed a candidate for a spot on a board of directors. The candidate appeared to have excellent credentials and much to contribute to the board. I asked, "How are your financial skills, such as reviewing financial statements?"

He thought for just a second and answered, "That would be a development area for me. I have done basic departmental budgeting, but I haven't worked with full organization-level financial statements."

My reaction? Great answer! Honest! Genuine! Respectful! It's what I expected, given what I knew of the candidate's work experience.

The result? The candidate was awarded a seat on the board, side by side with a skilled financial executive, who took the second open spot!

➔ QUESTION 9: WHAT HAPPENED AT YOUR PREVIOUS EMPLOYER (if you didn't leave of your own accord)?

If you've ever been "fired," "let go," "asked to leave," or whatever euphemism you want to call it, this might be the toughest question you'll face. It's tough to admit something didn't work out. You might feel embarrassed to have momentarily lost control of your career. And you could worry that the interviewer will regard this episode (and more?) as a failure. In my years of executive search, I've learned this is the question candidates most fear.

I understand. Your feelings are valid. But I'm going to coach you away from letting your feelings dictate how you answer this question.

FIRST INSTINCT: Many people ask me whether they need to admit they were fired. I'm well aware it's possible to fudge on your response. You wouldn't have to outright lie to make the situation sound a bit less severe, right? In other words, "Can't I just gloss over the fact that I was asked to leave?" "Can't I say I left on my own?" "Could I say I was caught up in a mass layoff?"

No, no, and no. I don't recommend you ever answer this question with even the tiniest amount of dishonesty or fabrication. It's just not worth it. You could slant the exact reason for your departure. Or you could misrepresent your departure date. Many people in job transition represent themselves as being employed as long as they're getting severance. Being on a severance plan, I feel compelled to remind you, isn't the same as being actively employed and on payroll.

As a leader, however, you rise and fall with your integrity. Seize this opportunity to demonstrate integrity by the grace and honesty with which you answer this question.

UNINTENDED RESULT: At the least, a dishonest answer has a vibe that causes interviewers discomfort. At worst, the entirety of your dishonest answer will be found out. Either way, you'll come across as lacking in integrity.

Dishonesty is dishonesty, whether it's the Yahoo CEO fabricating a computer science degree or you bending the truth about a job exit. When dishonesty about the true nature of a departure becomes known, the consequences are often brutal. I've seen candidates asked to withdraw from a search. I've seen job offers rescinded at the smallest hint of dishonesty. I've even seen a new executive asked to resign after only three months on the job when details emerged about his departure from a previous employer.

You should assume that the following facts can be easily uncovered through a background check, employment verification, credit check, reference check, or even good old Google:

- All your dates of employment
- Your date of college graduation
- The circumstances of your exit from previous employers (entirely likely to emerge in formal and informal reference checks)
- Any issues (criminal history, financial mismanagement, etc.) that might appear in a thorough, professionally conducted background check

Assume that anything and everything you say can and might be checked for accuracy and truthfulness. Although it's far from certain your fib about being asked to leave a job would ever be discovered, there can be dire consequences if it is. Don't risk it!

A truthful answer is always best. However, there are preferable ways to provide that truthful answer.

DO THIS INSTEAD: **"The truth, the whole truth, and nothing but the truth" is your appropriate guideline here.** Be prepared to tell, as briefly as possible, what happened. As with addressing any potentially negative information about your previous employer, be as succinct and positive as possible.

CONSIDER THIS ANSWER: "My boss was really hard to work for. He was critical and overly demanding. I can offer several references who would say the same. There were several VPs of human resources before me, and none of them worked out either. After I left, a couple of other people in the department left as well. So, yeah, I got let go, but it wasn't as if I was the only one."

CONTRAST THE FOLLOWING BETTER OPTION: "I appreciate your asking about this. Obviously, as stated on my résumé, I left the RFG Company in September. My boss initiated discussions about my exit, based on our differing views of how to run the department. But I agreed with his thinking. I respect that, as CEO, he had the right to make the best staffing decisions for how he wanted to build his team. I learned a lot while I worked for that firm."

The first answer sounds petulant and resentful. Even if the negativity were okay (which it rarely is), the response lacks impact because it brings others down in an attempt to justify the termination. It raises the possibility the candidate might deem any potential new boss difficult and overly demanding. The answer sounds anything but resilient, a possible sign the individual isn't emotionally ready to start a new job.

The second answer sounds more genuine. It demonstrates how to support the business and decisions made by leadership even in the midst of difficult circumstances. It shows a candidate who is able to rise above a negative situation, reamaining professional rather than getting personal.

The victim mentality has never worked once in winning a job. As you anticipate this question in an interview, be aware of the emotions it will cause inside you. First, recognize that as soon as an interviewer asks you this question, you'll likely experience some level of an automatic emotional response. You've feared this question all along, and here it is, as if it's being tossed in your face. Take a deep breath! Second, recognize that the adrenaline rush you feel can make you prone to over-explaining the most minute of details. The more you talk, the less believable you become. Anticipate and plan accordingly.

➔ QUESTION 10: WHAT DO YOU DO IN YOUR FREE TIME? (What do you do for fun?)

FIRST INSTINCT: You might be tempted to fib about hobbies in an effort to create the "right" impression, claiming interests you believe would connect with the interviewer (what executive doesn't love to golf?). The assumption is that a particular response will build rapport. Alternatively, you might be tempted to tell the interviewer you're so dedicated to your work that you have no free time left for outside activities.

UNINTENDED RESULT: Faux hobbies might come across as real, depending upon your storytelling skills. But remember: You're still in the recruitment process. How will you describe yourself to the *next* interviewer? What if you claim you love downhill skiing and the next person's office is decorated with horse-riding memorabilia? And what will your references say about you? How will you backtrack if you call yourself a serial globetrotter only to have one of your references call you a homebody and say she admires how you use your vacations to help family and friends?

If you're tempted to say you have no time for hobbies, remember that most organizations value what you bring to the job as a whole person. Most executives realize that outside activities energize us and create valuable new experiences that make us better people.

DO THIS INSTEAD: **Be yourself. Your own unique self. Nothing more or less.** Keep in mind that this question is usually well intentioned, almost always just a sincere attempt to get to know you.

Unless your interests are controversial, politically charged, or something you're embarrassed to share, by all means mention them. Sports, family activities, artistic or musical endeavors, educational programs, and the like are typical answers and come across just fine. Board or committee work, civic commitments, or volunteer activities are very much worth sharing. If you've gained new skills or expertise, mention that! It demonstrates your willingness to learn and challenge yourself. The candidate who took up the saxophone at age 50 was pretty memorable.

What about personal details? How much should you say? Use your best judgment, but again, these questions are usually just innocent ways of making conversation or getting to know you. You're under no obligation to divulge personal or family details, of course, but feel free to share basic information if you're so inclined. You might feel most comfortable sharing details in the context of outside interests and activities. For example, you might not offer up the bare comment, "I have two elementary school-aged sons." But you might frame it up this way: "My two sons enjoy baseball, and I've been their coach the last couple of years."

➜ QUESTION 11: THE TRICK QUESTION.

Everyone wants to know how to answer a trick question. My first response is that actual *trick* questions are rare. There are, however, *stupid* questions, *funny* questions, *misguided* questions, and *eccentric* questions. For example, one organization I worked with insisted on asking candidates, "What shape is a manhole cover?" Answer: "Round." A friend shared that she was asked in an interview, "If you were a car, what type would you be?" I suppose the question gets at the taste of the candidate. My friend said, "Cadillac."

I've never heard a client pitch a question to deliberately trick candidates. Questions that might be perceived as tricky are likely intended (rightly or wrongly) to gain insight into a candidate's personality—to evoke sense of humor or observe the approach to a question he or she couldn't possibly have prepared for. Or the interviewer may simply have heard from elsewhere, "Hey, this question might sound crazy, but it really works!"

So an interviewer might throw out an offbeat question not to be mean but to add humor to or alter the tempo of a serious interview. There often isn't a right or wrong answer. It might be a matter of taste or opinion. Don't get worried or hung up.

Consider these examples:

QUESTION: "What type of animal most exemplifies your leadership style?"

FIRST INSTINCT: "That question makes no sense." "That question has nothing to do with the job!" "What are you trying to get at?"

UNINTENDED RESULT: You could be seen as humorless, inflexible, or even rigid. You look unwilling to give the questioner the benefit of the doubt.

DO THIS INSTEAD: "Hmmm. I'd say a dog. There are lots of dog breeds, and I try to employ a variety of leadership approaches to match the situation."

Or

"An owl. My most recent role as dean of the School of Psychology required significant ongoing education to keep up with the new specialty degrees we were adding. I'd like to think that I can call myself *wise*."

QUESTION: "How many hours are there in a day?"

FIRST INSTINCT: "Ummmm, what are you getting at? Is this a trick question?"

UNINTENDED RESULT: You might sound brittle or unwilling to have a little fun in an otherwise serious process.

DO THIS INSTEAD: "Well, there are never enough, but 24 is all I get!"

Of course, there are tricky questions that are just badly worded inquiries. Go ahead and ask the interviewer to clarify.

→ QUESTION 12: DO YOU HAVE ANY QUESTIONS FOR ME?

I could write a book on this topic alone, because the questions that *you* ask in an interview make an enormous difference in how you're perceived. I've seen candidates do a mediocre job answering the bulk of an interviewer's questions and then completely turn around the meeting with a captivating set of questions that lead to meaningful dialogue. I've also seen a CEO's top-rated candidate drop to the bottom after fumbling this question.

Most hiring entities put great emphasis on a candidate's performance during this portion of the interview—but not for the reasons you might think. Sure, the questions posed need to be reasonable and appropriate. But even more telling to the hiring executive is how the questions are asked and how the candidate listens to answers and follows up. After all, isn't that the stuff of work? Questions are asked, answered, clarified, countered, followed up—and how that interaction looks and feels is just as important as the material under discussion.

It's the Monday Morning Staff Meeting!

FIRST INSTINCT: You might be tempted to wow a hiring team with your sheer volume of questions. You might consider drafting a list to disseminate to interviewers. Think of how impressive you'll appear when, given the floor, you open your folio and pull out two pages of questions neatly printed in 12-point Times Roman font. More is better, right?

UNINTENDED RESULT: **More isn't better! More is more! Better is better!** The main thing an impossibly long list of questions communicates is poor time management. The interviewer posing the question probably said something like, "We have a few minutes left today, so we'd like to turn it over to you for any questions you have for us." If your next move is to pull out a couple of pages of written questions to address in those "few minutes," your interviewer picks up a pen and jots down "time management concern."

The second thing conveyed by an excessive set of questions is a poor ability to prioritize. Picturing the Monday Morning Staff Meeting, how would you decide what to ask about a pressing issue? How would you filter your list knowing the Q&A protocol is a session with just enough time for a few key questions? Anything more than a handful of high-quality questions would come across as poor planning. You wouldn't be well served by a mash-up of strategic and tactical, general and specific, quick clarifications and topics requiring deeper exploration.

An executive knows what to ask and when to ask it. An executive realizes there's never enough time to air every question in a single meeting. The good news? In an executive-level hiring process, there's rarely just one session.

DO THIS INSTEAD: The rule is this: Never ask a question unless you sincerely want or need to know the answer *and* you're sure the information isn't readily available elsewhere *and* the question is appropriate to this stage of the process. Plan your questions! ***What do I really need to know right now to decide if I take the next step in pursuing this opportunity?***

Let me point out that you're at a severe disadvantage if you've already decided a job is a perfect fit. Why? You'll find it next to impossible to generate questions meaningful for whatever stage you're at in the selection process. Put another way, if you've already concluded that this job opportunity is "the one," you don't need to ask more questions to discern *whether* it's "the one." Here's what I see happen: Candidates who think a job is perfect skip over necessary, appropriate, thought-provoking questions. They play it safe. They avoid tough issues to minimize any possibility of upsetting the interviewer and ending their candidacy.

There's an obvious problem with playing it safe. Other candidates, who haven't decided this is the perfect job, come prepared with interesting, provocative, *real* questions. Not tons of questions, and none that shows any intent other than to help both parties decide whether this working relationship would be the right fit. Again, isn't that what the Monday Morning Staff Meeting is all about? People have big decisions to make. They rightly expect give-and-take by everyone present as all attendees put relevant information on the table and deliberate with their very best judgment.

The interview is no different. A hiring organization expects the candidate to show up as a partner in a discernment process. Collaboration is the name of the game, and everyone expects the candidate to contribute questions that count.

And it doesn't end with delivering an insightful question. When others answer, listen carefully. You won't have to pretend their responses are important if the question *actually matters* to you. Maintain eye contact. Nod. Jot a note, if you need to. Thank the responder for the answer. Make a fol- low-up comment as needed. That's it. Don't overcomplicate it.

Composing questions

Your own questions should be uniquely prepared, but in a pinch, you can refer to these questions, which tend to work well:

ABOUT THE JOB:

- What are your primary objectives for this role?
- What could get in the way of achieving the objectives?
- What are the biggest challenges I would face in this position?
- At the end of the first year, how will success be measured in this position?
- Are any significant changes on the horizon that could impact the position as it's been presented?
- Where might I face difficulties, and how would you suggest I prepare for the challenge?
- Where should I focus attention during my first 90 days? (What needs to be done first?)
- What would you want me to keep about the way this job is currently being done? What changes would you recommend?

ABOUT THE BOSS:

- What is it like to work for _________ (boss's name)?
- What has she most recently praised you for?

ABOUT THE DEPARTMENT OR FUNCTION:

- How does this team work together?
- How is this group/team/department viewed by the rest of the organization?

ABOUT THE ORGANIZATION:

- How does this organization differentiate itself from similar organizations?
- Any specific question, such as "I've read the 990 and I would like to ask about . . ." Or "I've looked over your strategic plan. My question is . . ."

ABOUT THE CULTURE OR WORK ENVIRONMENT:

- What's it like to work here? What is the organizational culture?
- What has kept you here? (for a long-tenured employee)
- What made you join this organization? (for a new employee)
- How does this organization live up to its value of diversity and inclusion?
- What types of people tend to fit here and what types tend not to fit?
- What's this organization's approach to leadership development?

CHALLENGES AND OPPORTUNITIES:

- What one thing about the organization/function/department/job do you wish you'd known ahead of time?
- What keeps the leaders here awake at night?

NEVER ASK THIS QUESTION

There's one question I don't think you should ever ask. It's any variation of *"What do you think of me so far?"* or *"How did I do in this interview?"*

I recently watched from the back of the room as a corporate president interviewed a candidate for vice president. Things were going well. The potential new employee was articulate, and she responded with meaningful examples. The interview appeared to go quite smoothly right up to the end. The president made a few remarks to wrap things up, and then the two individuals stood up and shook hands. "Before I leave, I have one more question," the candidate said. "Sure, what's that?" the president replied. "How did I do? You know, compared with the other candidates?"

The room went silent as the president gathered his thoughts. He repeated his point about meeting with several candidates and making a decision within a week. "But," the VP candidate asked again, "I really want to know where I stand!"

Asking these questions displayed disrespect for the president's decision-making process and timeline. Repeating the question meant the candidate didn't notice or didn't care that the question had made the president uncomfortable.

That candidate didn't win the interview.

A better question? "Is there anything we discussed or in my background that you'd like me to address further?" You might get some helpful information, and the interviewer's response likely will be as much of a hint as you'll ever receive before a decision is finalized.

CHAPTER 24

NEVER DO THESE THINGS

WE'VE TALKED ABOUT a lot of *dos* for the interview, as well as a few don'ts. But there are also some additional definitive *don'ts!* The following behaviors, while not automatic derailers, are highly problematic in executive interviews. Further, they're relatively easy to avoid. So take a look. Do any of these challenging behaviors apply to you? Avoid them at all costs!

DON'T USE JARGON.

My recruitment schedule creates fascinating juxtapositions. I might interview a vice president in manufacturing one morning and, in the afternoon of the same day, a vice president from, say, actuarial science. As I anticipate interviewing candidates from large organizations, I worry a bit. I often consider padding the interview with extra minutes, enough to wade through company-specific terms and lingo. I also plan to grab an extra shot of coffee. All those insider acronyms! That mumbo jumbo is mind-numbing!

If you're coming from a large company, please hear my special shout of caution. Watch out! Anyone groomed in an organization with a strong culture learns a vernacular distinctive to that company. It rarely translates anywhere else. Your job is to make your background and language understandable to a *general audience*. One afternoon, for example, I interviewed two candidates for a position of division president. Both individuals hailed from large business-services organizations. As always, I needed to quickly ascertain each candidate's current place in the company, along with the size and scope of responsibilities. So I asked each a simple question:

How is your business organized?

THE FIRST CANDIDATE ANSWERED: "The company is divided into three sectors, CCM, ADM and SAM. I'm the general manager of the CCM sector. Because we're a matrix organization, I'm also co-leader of the western group and report to the Global BU SVP."

THE SECOND CANDIDATE ANSWERED: "The company is divided into three divisions, based on client investment size, in other words, small-, midsize, and large businesses. I lead the midsize division. I report to the president of U.S. operations."

I needed to ask each candidate follow-up questions to clarify, but which one gave me the most useful information right at the start? The second candidate apparently understood how to interact outside his organizational bubble. That first candidate seemed to communicate several things that concerned me:

- "I'm not able to pull myself away from company jargon." (Which only makes me wonder *why?* Can't she describe her company in general language?)
- "I think my use of the jargon will impress you." (Trust me, no one is impressed. We all have our own company lingo. It doesn't make you sound smarter.)
- "I'm going to answer in a way that's most comfortable for me; you figure it out." (Not an attitude I'm looking for.)

Do not—under any circumstances—use acronyms or other unique language that might not be known to the questioner. Don't throw in terms only used by a specific industry, trade group, company, or function. Do your utmost to make your answers meaningful to the questioner. When in doubt, ask, "Should I clarify any terms for you?"

The only exception to this rule is if the questioner shares your background closely and uses a technical word or phrase in the question itself. Then feel free to use that specific reference.

DON'T CRITICIZE YOUR FORMER EMPLOYER.

I frequently interview executives who work for well-known bosses, some of whom are famously difficult. I'm always impressed by an executive who has the self-control, respect, and judgment to avoid speaking badly of a boss, even one whose leadership flaws are legendary from break rooms to boardrooms.

One candidate vying for an executive director position had worked for a CEO who was widely known to be difficult. In response to any number of questions, the candidate could have made subtle or overt references to his superior's, *ahem*, challenging approach. Instead, he focused on his own work. His references later told me that the candidate was a positive and healing presence for other staff beaten down by this CEO. All of us in the interview process gave the candidate high marks for focusing on his own contributions versus the limitations of others. He got the job.

Don't ever criticize anyone. Ever. No matter how justified you think you are. There are two sides to every story, and good leaders recognize that talking negatively about people who aren't present to defend themselves is fundamentally unfair and unwise. Moreover, keep in mind that interviewers *always represent the employer.* If you use an interview to bad-mouth previous employers, your listeners will wonder if someday you'll stab *them* in the back.

An executive candidate recently mentioned in a group interview that her prior CEO had installed cameras around the offices to make sure employees "didn't steal office supplies!" This had gone on for years. Everyone chuckled at the draconian boss. But the negative comments raised questions: *Why did you stay there so long? Couldn't you get hired somewhere else?*

When interviewers ask about former employers, offer a balanced perspective. The mere act of interviewing means you've disconnected from the organization for some reason. It might be negative. Take pains to fill in the positive. What did you enjoy about your experience there? What did you learn?

Being asked about a previous employer can be a ticking bomb for candidates who haven't worked through potential anger or bitterness about why they exited their former job. They think they have their emotions under control until a question unleashes a spew of negativity. Criticizing others in the interview context shows poor judgment. Not a characteristic valued in the Monday Morning Staff Meeting!

DON'T CRITICIZE THE HIRING ORGANIZATION.

What? Bad-mouth the company you're seeking to join? Did I misspeak? Who would do that? As it turns out, plenty of candidates head down that road. I repeatedly see it play out in a couple of scenarios.

First, some candidates criticize a hiring organization in an attempt to look knowledgeable. A candidate once told the CEO of an agricultural credit union, "You have an excessive number of farmers on your board of directors." (What's "excessive"?

Compared with what or whom? Does this statement have any relevance to your interest in the job?) If this were a genuine concern, the comment could be rephrased with a more respectful tone: "How do you determine your board makeup? Do you think you have the right mix at this time?"

Someone else suggested a CEO's organization must be "limping along" and having "real trouble" because an interim CFO was in place. Indeed, the interim was very strong and was bringing great value to the organization.

I've never understood the reasoning behind these uncomplimentary remarks. I suppose they come from a misguided hope that the hiring executive will think, *Wow! I never thought of that! This guy really sees our blind spots! Maybe we should hire him to help us fix them!*

Second, some candidates criticize a hiring entity when I pass along less-than-positive feedback or bad news. Candidates might speak glowingly about an opportunity, the staff they've met, their outlook on the job and the organization's prospects. However, when I call to say they didn't make the cut, their demeanor instantly crashes. I've heard a hundred times, "Well, if *they* don't think I'm the top candidate, then *they* don't know what they're doing. *They* must not value great leadership or my contacts in the industry." And so on and so on. It's disappointing when a recruitment process stalls, requires an extra step, or reorders priorities for the position, but I urge you to bite your tongue before you criticize the hiring entity. You're a professional. You understand that sometimes organizational needs change. What if you're reconsidered and invited back for further meetings? Can you expect people to rally behind you despite your negativity? How can you take back your harsh words?

Criticism never advances your cause. And even indirect disparagements are picked up loud and clear. Whatever criticism you pose as a candidate is likely based on limited information. You can't know the history behind a decision, the trade-offs considered, the political realities, plans already in place, etc. You can't know everything happening inside the organization. Even recruiters often can't. My advice? Watch your words!

DON'T NAME-DROP.

I loathe name-dropping. There. I said it. When someone brings up prominent people they've met ("Did I tell you I met Senator Bigworth?") or mentions executives I'm *supposed* to know ("You worked at IBM; did you ever meet John Akers?"), well, I don't like it. Do you? I'm certain that most people dislike name-dropping. From my observations, they especially dislike it at interviews, where crucial first impressions are formed.

I was participating in a video interview when an exceptionally well-qualified candidate was asked what leadership style he admired. The candidate paused, then launched in. "Well, back when I worked at Hart/Graves in Phoenix," he said, "I had a terrific boss. Morty Schulz. He was a hoot! Morty and the purchasing VP—what was his name again? Oh yes! Sven Johansson. They were terrific guys. Sven's last name was actually pronounced Yo-hanson, like with a Y. Any- way, the three of us . . ." On and on he went, throwing in names of plenty of other executives at that organization and telling random stories.

The candidate was having a ball reliving fond memories. I sat bewildered. Sure enough, the client feedback said this well-qualified candidate seemed "egocentric." Their word. They couldn't quite put a finger on it, but the exchange left them feeling the candidate might not fit their more inclusive culture.

Candidates think, *If I toss out some big names it will reflect well on me.* Name-dropping is often a last-ditch effort to make an impression. Ironically, it can be perceived as desperate or elitist, and neither is an attractive quality in a leader. I had a candidate who was told flat out that one reason he wasn't selected was that flaunting his connections was off-putting.

DON'T SHARE CONFIDENTIAL INFORMATION.

You might assume I'm just talking about items covered by nondisclosure agreements and non-competes. I'm not. A general-manager candidate was interviewing at a transportation firm. When asked about his skills in developing people, he mentioned his service director, PeggyLynn. "You know how it is with parents," he said. "They tell their kids to pick things up, and the kids don't do it. So the mom does it for them. Well, PeggyLynn has three kids, and I think she brings that style to work. When her managers don't get their work done, she does it for them." Then he went on to describe his development efforts with her.

My mind spun. *These interviewers live in the same city as PeggyLynn. That's not a common name, and now the group knows her company and job title. What if one of the interviewers knows her? What if PeggyLynn is a friend or relative?*

See the problem? There's a wide range of confidential information that's not appropriate for public consumption. Don't share that your boss is having marital issues. Don't offer that your company owners may have IRS trouble—even if that's why you're exiting.

The same answer could have been delivered without

violating confidentiality. He could have provided the illustration without using her name. For example, "A person on my staff has issues with delegation, and I've worked with her on a development plan." Or "A person on my staff—let's call her Shondra—has had issues we're working on."

When the conference-room door closes behind and you head home, are you comfortable having said negative things about people you know? Could your words get back to those you've disparaged? What does it say about your ability to manage sensitive corporate information if you readily spill personal matters others expect you to keep private?

DON'T TAKE CONTROL OF THE MEETING.

I can't tell you how often I've had candidates come in for an interview only to have them try to take over the meeting. "Before we get started," they say, "I'd like to ask some questions." Or "I only have an hour, so I'd like to cover my most current experience first." I wish I was kidding, or even exaggerating. But I've seen it happen. Apply the filter of the Monday Morning Staff Meeting and consider how this behavior comes across. A CEO immediately imagines the candidate arriving at the CEO's meeting and hijacking the agenda, or demanding that the group change the original plan for the session. How could giving this impression possibly help you get hired?

The hiring entity called the meeting—whether the arrangements were made by the human resources director, the CEO, the board of directors, or someone working on their behalf. In any case, *you're not in charge*. Therefore, let the other party run the meeting. **Whoever calls the meeting runs the meeting. That's true for all meetings, and never more true than in a job interview.**

DON'T ASK OTHERS TO MANAGE YOU.

I've seen people cry in interviews. I've seen people yell. I've seen people pound the table in rage. Still, one of the worst interview behaviors is a bit more subtle but no less harmful. It happens far more often than you'd think. It sounds like this:

- "I tend to talk a lot, so you'll need to stop me if I go on too long."
- "I'm a person of few words, so my answers will be short and you'll probably have to ask me follow-up questions on everything."
- "I don't have a great sense of time, so you'll have to watch the time and let me know if we need to speed up."

With comments such as these, you are abdicating your own self-management to the interviewer, making the other person responsible for you. It's not appropriate for any job seeker, much less a candidate vying for a leadership role.

No matter what role you want to win, the ability to manage yourself is essential. Asking the interviewer to take responsibility for your behavior is my number-one pet peeve and a true no-no.

CHAPTER 25

AFTER THE INTERVIEW

PETRA EXITED HER INTERVIEW WITH THE CEO OF BYHRAM NASH FEELING PLEASED. The moment she was alone behind the wheel of her car, she allowed herself to express her thoughts out loud: "That was a really good conversation!" Deonne was pushing forward with an impressive strategic plan. Petra left eager to be part of facing industry challenges head on. She pictured teaming up with Deonne as easily as they had fallen into their give-and-take conversation. And she was surprised how much she liked the individual who might be her next boss. And to think she was at first reluctant to consider this opportunity!

Petra reminded herself not to let her hopes get the best of her—for now. At the moment, she needed to follow up the meeting with a thank-you note of some sort. Because the hiring decision would be made soon, expediency was probably more important than a handwritten note, so Petra chose to send an email thank-you to Deonne, copying Murray and the executive search firm.

Petra expressed gratitude for the consideration of her candidacy. She highlighted areas where she thought her background fit the role well. Lastly, she remarked on her positive observations of the organization's culture and her desire to join their team and help them grow.

After hitting the send button, Petra also sent a quick note

to update a friend who had consulted at Byhram Nash and encouraged Petra to pursue the opportunity.

Tomorrow Petra would debrief with the recruiter at Wynn & Zehring. She shot off an email to confirm that phone appointment, then called it a day.

CHAPTER 26

YOUR POST-INTERVIEW STEPS

RECRUITERS KNOW ONE THING FOR SURE: There's a reverse correlation between how well candidates think they performed in interviews and how well they were actually perceived.

Consider these conversations:

> **RECRUITER:** How do you think the interview went?
> **CANDIDATE 1:** I nailed it. I answered all of the questions, and we actually talked for 15 minutes longer than scheduled. Everyone seemed really nice. I'm excited about this job. Yup! I think I aced the interview.

Now, contrast this response:

> **RECRUITER:** How do you think the interview went?
> **CANDIDATE 2:** Well, everyone seemed really nice. And I answered all of the questions. Hmmm, I think I could have given more detail about my pro bono legal work. And I think my example of my best organizational culture fell a bit flat. Talking about an international setting didn't seem to correlate as well as I'd thought it would. I

know I' ll come up with other things I could have done better. But I hope it went well from their perspective!

I can almost guarantee the hiring organization will give unfavorable feedback about Candidate 1. Conversely, I would bet my house that Candidate 2 will receive great reviews. How can I be so sure? I' ve seen these reactions and counterreactions *thousands* of times.

What's different about the second response? Why will that person almost certainly be invited back? Well, which candidate sounds more reflective? Which probably gave more thoughtful answers (answering the "question behind the question")? Which was more likely to manage time well? And if neither candidate gets the job, which do you think will perform better in the next interview?

The candidate who is more self-critical after the first interview will reflect, draw conclusions, and apply those lessons in subsequent rounds. If my humble statistics hold true, that candidate will probably land this job—or finish first next time.

Reflect, learn and plan

After the interview, take time to reflect as soon as you can on these points:

- **What went well?** Why did that part work? What did the interviewer say or do to give you that impression? Did he or she nod, smile, or indicate verbal agreement? How sure are you?
- **What didn't go so well?** Why do you think that? Did the interviewer signal that your answer or the discussion

wasn't going well? Did the interviewer glance at the clock, interrupt you, redirect your answer?

Recalling what went well, determine what you'll carry into future interviews. At points that didn't go well, make a list of what you've learned. What can you do differently next time? How will you make sure you do things differently? Could you practice, brainstorm alternative examples, talk through sticking points? A trusted and honest advisor could give feedback on portions of the interview where you're simply not sure how you came across.

After you've reflected, create a mini action plan for future interviews. Don't shortchange this part of the process! For any given position, you'll probably participate in multiple interviews. Make each one better than the last by purposefully reflecting, learning, and planning for improvements.

When you've finished debriefing, it's time to let go. Soon enough you'll learn how things turned out. Regardless of the outcome, congratulate yourself on a great effort. You did your best. You learned from the experience. You'll do even better next time. And that is something to feel good about.

You almost never get a do-over after an interview. An interview is a one-shot deal. I'm sorry to say it, but you get one chance to make an impression and answer whatever questions come your way. Like a major sales presentation or any key business interaction, an interview presents one opportunity to impress. When you're told you're no longer a candidate, you need to sit tight. Never call an interviewer back to share more positive attributes about yourself or to offer more examples of your fit.

Should you ever reconnect with an interviewer to do damage control? If something happened that you truly can't leave unaddressed, go ahead and contact the interviewer. It won't likely change the outcome, but you'll feel better. For example, let's say you interviewed for a position with a company you've done business with. You made the terrible mistake of talking badly about a former boss. Worse, you used the person's name. Driving home, you feel sick. It's too late to unsay your remarks, and you might spend a sleepless night tossing and turning and reflecting on your behavior.

In an instance like that, go ahead and contact the interviewer. Describe the situation as you recall it, state your apology for a situation poorly handled, and finish the communication on a positive note, such as remarking that you enjoyed the opportunity to meet with the interviewer.

Again, there's little chance you'll change the interview outcome, but you'll feel better. You'll head off a potentially embarrassing future encounter with the interviewer. That's appropriate and admirable.

Follow-up strategies

What's the protocol for interview follow-ups? These days, an email thank-you is usually appropriate and sufficient. If you believe the hiring team will make decisions quickly, send an email within 24 hours. If you're the first to be interviewed among several candidates over the course of weeks, you've got a bit more time. Consider sending your thank-you later as a way to stay top of mind.

On occasion, you might use your thank-you to clarify a response. Such as, "After further reflection on our discussion about scaling into an overseas market, I feel it's important to mention that scaling product overseas was one component of my role as a general manager at TNC." However, don't ever turn your thank-you note into a sell job about your qualifications. Write your note with the purpose of expressing gratitude and ongoing interest.

Make your words personal and special for the receiver. For example, mention a unique remark or insightful moment from the interview. Comment on a common interest that came up. You could include a positive remark about the interview experience and restate your interest in continuing in the recruitment process.

If you interviewed with multiple people in separate meetings, I suggest sending each interviewer an individual thank-you note. Try to express distinct comments to each. In a real pinch, you could send one message to multiple people, but I see that as a lesser option. Yet, a group thank-you is better than no thank-you.

> **Thanking interviewers can be a point of differentiation, but it won't work miracles.** A gracious follow-up note goes in the "plus" column, but it's never a decision-maker. I've never heard anyone say, "Jason isn't skilled, but let's hire him because he wrote a thank-you note."

The waiting game

You've survived the phone screen. You've enjoyed what felt like a successful interview. With hope in your heart, you've sent appropriate thanks. You've waited one week for a response, then two, then three. You've left a breezy voicemail for your contact and waited yet another week. *What's taking so long?* Should you continue to follow up?

The discomfort of waiting is tough. It feels like an eternity between an interview and hearing about a next step. You might think it's odd, perhaps bordering on rude, that a hiring entity doesn't respond quickly.

Can I offer an insight? You're forgetting what it's like on the other side of the process. I've seen countless factors slow a hiring process. Most are just ordinary, deliberate steps of a high-stakes executive hiring decision. There may be multiple candidates to interview. A leader might appreciate time to reflect on the fit of a slate of candidates. If multiple interviewers took part, the organization almost always pauses to consolidate those impressions. That means coordinating all of those individual schedules, which takes time!

And there's life, of course. Work travel. Unexpected projects. Vacations. Sick kids. Sometimes interviewers just aren't able to respond as quickly as planned.

When you're in the day-to-day commotion of a workplace, you likely don't give those waiting for a response a second thought. When you're on the outside hoping for the smallest tidbit of news, your head goes to all kinds of unproductive places.

Even those who have extensive hiring experience can't really project what a hiring organization "should" do. You can't dwell on what you regard as HR best practices. You're not on the hiring team. This isn't your decision. I've worked with hundreds of hiring organizations, and I've never seen any two follow identical hiring procedures. The process is out of your hands.

Acknowledging those realities nevertheless suggests a burning question: How often should you follow up with the hiring organization? My general advice is *once*. If you've waited longer than you were told, it's appropriate to follow up with a brief email or a quick call to the organization, or to the executive search firm. After that, I honestly don't think it serves you well to continue reaching out. While it can be nothing short of maddening to wait, most of the time there are reasonable, appropriate explanations for the holdup. Unfortunately, the explanations often aren't appropriate to share with candidates.

Continuing to ask the hiring organization where things are at doesn't help move things along.

As you await word on whether you'll progress in the hiring process, your best play is to wait graciously and professionally. One follow-up is appropriate. Two check-ins might be understandable. Three or more? That's being a pest. Maybe even perceived as aggressive. Be patient. It will pay off.

I understand that what I just shared likely isn't what you want to hear. If you're out of work or in some other high-risk scenario and desperately need to land a new role, please hear this next word of advice. It may be among the most important messages I could ever give you: Do everything in your power to pivot to your next job search task. If you have an ounce of energy to fret about a hiring process that feels slow or opaque, you have enough energy for other activities that will actually advance your search. There are far better ways to use your time than investing energy in something you can do nothing about.

What do I mean by "pivot"? If you're broken up about one interview, I have no doubt there's a list of other things you ought to be doing to find your next role. Are you serious about moving forward? Get busy. You've got networking meetings to schedule and maximize. Work on your Job Match Matrix to better explain your skills. Attend industry gatherings and reach out to recruiters. Expand your social media presence and thought leadership to boost your chance of getting noticed. Don't neglect learning opportunities to backfill gaps that surface in interviews.

The more things you have going on, the greater your array, and the less you'll obsess over a single opportunity, no matter how promising it looks. Instead of waiting for that phone call or email, you'll be so busy expanding your pipeline of jobs—working on this, that, and the other thing—that you won't get hung up over one position. If you turn your ner- vous energy into action, you'll feel better. Ultimately, you'll achieve better results.

Occasionally you'll interview for a job (even an executive role) and never hear from the hiring organization again. It's a terrible practice. It hurts you as a high-quality candidate more than words can say. But organizations sometimes drop the ball inadvertently. It's all the more reason to immediately pivot your attention to job-search work that leads you to other opportunities.

Another offer

I can think of one exception to my advice about ***not*** reaching back to a hiring organization more than once (or maybe twice). **If you have a verbal or written job offer from another organization, you're free to call and inform the first organization of the offer and explain your interest in pursuing a job there.** Ask if an accelerated timeline for a decision is possible. A call could go like this:

> "Hello, Mim. This is Poppi Hines. I've so appreciated getting to know you and Nocco Inc. I'm truly interested in the role of quality assurance manager. However, I want to let you know that I've received a job offer from Washburn Edison. I'm not sure if there is any possibility for an accelerated process to continue to evaluate my candidacy, but I wanted to make you aware. Based on what I know about the two jobs, I am somewhat more interested in the job at Nocco than the job that was offered at Washburn Edison. I have a week to let Washburn Edison know my decision."

Don't ever make up an offer elsewhere just to get back in front of a company you like. This situation relates only when you have a real, live job offer in hand.

If the organization can't accommodate your request and make a quick decision about your candidacy, at least you tried. On the other hand, a quick turnaround could happen. I've seen many hiring organizations move with surprising alacrity rather than risk lose their top candidate.

Withdrawing from interviewing

If something happens that impacts your ability to accept the position as presented or perform the duties as required, speak up immediately.

Suppose you're considering a highly intriguing job at a nonprofit organization. Although the salary is in line with similar jobs in the sector, it pays significantly less than what you've been making. With your spouse's income, however, you can afford the cut in pay. The day after setting up the interview, however, your spouse is laid off. Suddenly you can't consider taking a job at a lower salary. The right move is to withdraw from the process. Don't proceed with the interview, counting on those good-hearted folks to love you so much that an extra $50,000 in annual salary will magically appear.

Things happen. Don't wait. Call right away. Explain your circumstance. Apologize. Don't forget that people hire people. When you approach a situation with honesty and authenticity, you can get through almost anything.

CHAPTER 27

THE OFFER

MURRAY SMILED. Filling an important organizational hole always felt like a major win, ***assuming that openings don't happen too often,*** he thought, ***and that roles come open for the right reasons.***

For one last time, Murray scanned Petra Begay's formal offer letter. The terms he had recommended to Deonne quickly gained her approval, and within hours he'd crafted this document offering Petra the position of vice president of sales and marketing.

The leadership team at Byhram Nash felt an urgency to get the right person into this role, but Murray cautioned them to expect a brief lag as the process concluded. No matter how attractive, an offer was almost always met with a request for a few days to look over the agreement and discuss it with others whose opinion matters. Many candidates had questions about benefits, and if Murray couldn't provide answers, the director of benefits administration would step in to clarify.

Murray also factored in time for some back-and-forth over compensation and benefits. *There's always negotiation. Always.* Murray would take the lead in discussions, consulting with Deonne only if there were significant changes. Murray always felt a little unease before a deal was done, but he reminded himself that his success rate with extending offers and landing candidates topped 95 percent.

By the time this executive hiring process culminated in an

offer, Deonne and others were excited, even anxious, about getting Petra to join the company. And, as always, Murray looked forward to being the conduit for a candidate saying yes.

He finished the offer letter and cover sheet. *Almost there*.

A few days later . . .

"High five!" Deonne and Murray slapped hands. Murray had received the signed offer letter from Petra Begay, with a tentative start date in four weeks. Murray could check off a crucial HR project. Deonne had every reason to believe they were bringing the right leader on board. She was confident Petra knew the marketplace and would be a capable executive. With a major strategy retreat scheduled six weeks out, the timing was ideal to add Petra's perspective to the mix.

"You know," Deonne said to Murray. "Executive hiring isn't an easy process, but this was as good as it gets. An outcome like this makes it all worthwhile."

CHAPTER 28

WHAT DOES WINNING LOOK LIKE?

I RECEIVED AN EMAIL ONE MORNING FROM SOMEONE WHO SAID, "I JUST WANT TO LET YOU KNOW THAT I CAME IN SECOND AGAIN. Please keep me in mind." This individual had finished in second place several times. She'd been looking to move up to executive director, a role I have no doubt she'll fill with great success. She runs a huge division of an enormous nonprofit, with something like 600 people reporting to her. In an earlier stint in state government, she skillfully managed 1000.

If you're not chosen for one job, remember that it's one job. What have you learned? Well, you've likely learned something. Missing out on a role you want isn't fun, but you can probably pick yourself up and try again.

Occasionally I do come across people who are terribly underqualified for everything they apply for. They've got trouble with self-understanding and fit, and have a hard time assessing what jobs are right for them. I'm less concerned that's your situation, given that you've made the effort to read to the end of a book about presenting yourself well in interviews. I'm confident you've caught my message about matching your skills to a role, as well as what I've said about the ultimate importance of fit, that dynamic I've called the

Monday Morning Staff Meeting.

If you have a string of interviews where you're not selected, your frustration likely will grow. At that point, my advice is to team up with a career coach. A qualified coach can help you discern what's behind your near misses. You need to process with a professional who is not your spouse, not your buddy, not anyone inclined to say, "You're a perfect fit!" for all opportunities. You also don't want to get lost in your own perspective on the situation because it is incredibly difficult to coach yourself.

My strong recommendation is to consult with someone who does this all the time, who has helped hundreds or even thousands of high-quality people land in best-fit roles. Someone like that can help you troubleshoot every step of the job-search process. A coach can be a sounding board to practice answering tough questions, a dispassionate assessor of areas where you need extra preparation, and a mirror that reflects how you appear at interviews.

Whatever you do, don't go through this process alone.

Winning

This book is called *Winning the Executive Interview*. What does it mean to "win an interview"?

An interview might result in the job offer you hope for. But that doesn't always happen. Keep an open mind. There are many ways to win.

The most common way to think about a win in the context of a job interview is to win the job—in other words, to get the offer and take it. If at the end of the interview process, you're at the "highly interested" end of the continuum, this is indeed a very desirable outcome.

However, other things can transpire during an interview process that I would also consider a win.

If you have an open mind, another way to win is getting

an offer for a job other than the one you're competing for. Not long ago, a client interviewing candidates for a COO position liked the top two equally well. The team literally couldn't make up their minds. Until they realized they might not have to. There was also a sales VP role open at the company, and one of the COO candidates brought a strong sales background. With a bit of creativity and a slight tweak of the sales role, they offered the COO position to one candidate and SVP of sales to the other. Everyone won!

An interview might not result in a new job but could morph into a different category of ongoing business relationship. A top candidate for a president position in the electronic-parts industry had navigated multiple interviews and ranked as one of the top two candidates. A deeper look at her existing non-compete agreement showed the language was very comprehensive. By taking a new job, she could well be in violation, and she didn't care to spend the next several months fighting a legal battle. She respectfully withdrew from the process. By then, however, she had made a thoroughly positive impression on the CEO. While she didn't win a new job, a relationship had been forged. She and the CEO stayed in touch, and their companies joined forces on a number of projects over the next few years.

Many of my client organizations send out project work. They need consultants. They want partners. If you're laser focused on a full-time permanent executive position as your only acceptable outcome, that's great. Stay focused. It never works to say, "Hey, I'll take anything," because that's almost never true. Anything? Really? But if you've been authentic, sharp, and articulate, winning could look different from what you ever expected. Maybe even better.

There should be another win that you take away from virtually any interview: a connection that lasts beyond this interaction. One client of mine, a consulting firm, has hired me a few times over the years to find leaders. I stand in awe at what

I've watched unfold. The company has stayed in touch with virtually every candidate it has interviewed over the years, getting together for coffee, lunch, and ongoing conversation. Imagine the value of a consulting company staying connected with a broad network of talented individuals. Put yourself in the shoes of past interviewees who could have stomped away angry or upset at not being chosen for the job. Instead, they've ended up as friends and supporters of the organization.

I have to chalk up this remarkable practice to the consultancy's unique culture. But my hope is that the experience of interviewing will win you something similar—that you have an authentic human interaction with each person you meet, and that you somehow commit to each other's mutual good.

While you can't control how your interviewers might react, as a candidate you can graciously reach out with thanks to each for the opportunity to meet and learn more about their work. Hang on to their contact information. Reach out to them occasionally (as you should with everyone in your network). Not to inquire about whether they've got a gig available; just to update them on your latest and wish them well. You might even finish your note with my surprising networking question, "What can I do to help you?"

LinkedIn is currently the tool of choice to establish lasting connections in real time. At Ballinger|Leafblad, we have the perspective that almost no LinkedIn contact is a bad contact. (Some colleagues in my field, surprisingly, have the completely opposite perspective.) My suggestion is that you send a quick note with an invitation to connect on LinkedIn to any person with whom you interview. Immediacy is crucial. Send the note on the day you meet, and the person is considerably more likely to link with you. Or even the day before. ("I look forward to seeing you tomorrow," and, just like that, you're connected.)

My suggestion to stay connected has a pragmatic basis, one that could someday help you win your interview. People who hire turn to their networks (especially via LinkedIn) more and more. Why engage an expensive recruiter or pay to place an ad when they can dig into their connections and say, "Director of supply chain, who do I talk to about that?" You never know what might come around.

Is this crazy? I don't think so. What I'm describing is how life is supposed to work. In the grand scheme of things, it is how hiring should work. It's all about people finding a match to do good work together. If you don't find that at one organization, in time you will at another. Just don't give up.

In the meantime, until you do win your interview, keep growing and applying your unique skills to make this world a better place. I wish you all the best.

Marcia Ballinger

Marcia Ballinger, PhD

Website: www.ballingerleafblad.com
Linkedin: linkedin.com/in/marciaballinger
Facebook: https://www.facebook.com/BLSearch/
Twitter: @marciaballinger

PART 3

APPENDIX: AT-HAND INTERVIEW WORKSHEETS

Your Objective at Each Step of the Process

Interviews are exercises in discernment for hiring organizations as well as candidates. Winning candidates don't rush the process. Nor do they lag behind.

Remember your key goal at each significant turn:

☐ **PAPER APPLICATION:**

To be noticed among many applicants, and be invited to your first conversation

☐ **PHONE SCREEN:**

To answer questions that probe your feasibility and viability
If you're still interested in the role, your objective is to be invited to an in-person interview.

☐ **FIRST-ROUND INTERVIEW:**

To get a sense of the job and the organization
If you're still interested in the role, your objective is to be invited to the next round of interviews.

☐ SECOND/FINAL INTERVIEW:

To determine if the job is truly a good fit—and whether you would take the job if you were offered it
If you're still interested in the role, your objective is to get an offer.

☐ OFFER REVIEW:

To determine if the offer matches your understanding of the compensation package from prior discussions
If not, ask questions and engage in further discussion.

When the answer is yes, accept the offer!

Phone-screen Prep—Check these Things Before the Call

- [ ] Is your phone battery charged?

- [ ] Are you in a quiet place?

- [ ] Will you be undisturbed for the duration of the call?

- [ ] **HAVE THESE HANDY:**

  Résumé
  Job Match Matrix
  Pen and paper

- [ ] **KNOW THE FOLLOWING:**

  Name of person you'll be speaking with?

  ____

  What is this person's title?

  ____

  What is this person's role in the recruitment process?

  ____

AT THE END OF THE PHONE INTERVIEW, ASK THESE QUESTIONS:

What is the next step?

____

____

____

____

Do you have a sense of timing?

____

____

How would you prefer that I follow up?

____

____

____

____

Who should I direct any questions to?

____

____

FINALLY:
Say thank you (for the interviewer's interest, for the great questions, for the engaging dialogue, for the opportunity, for whatever makes sense for your situation)!

Job Match Matrix

QUALIFICATION/ REQUIREMENT	MY EXPERIENCE/RESULTS

MY NARRATIVE/RATING

Pre-Interview Quick Check

INTERVIEW LOGISTICS:

- ☐ I know the interview location and how to get there.
- ☐ I know where to park.
- ☐ I've double-checked the start time of my interview.
- ☐ I know how long the interview will last.
- ☐ I know the names and titles of the interviewers.
- ☐ I've done basic research on each interviewer.

ATTIRE:

- ☐ I know what I'm going to wear.
- ☐ My interview outfit is clean and pressed.

WHAT TO BRING:

- [ ] I've got a folio, paper, and pen.
- [ ] I've got extra copies of my résumé.

DISTRACTIONS:

- [ ] My phone is turned off.
- [ ] I'm not carrying a pager or any other distractions.

MINDSET:

- [ ] I can picture myself in the interview being clear, concise, positive, gracious—a success!

Pre-interview Self-talk

Spend a few minutes before the interview in a quiet spot.

- [ ] **Take several deep breaths.** Slow down.

- [ ] **Reflect.** If you're a spiritual person, you may wish to ask for guidance and wisdom during the meeting. Be grateful for this opportunity and be encouraged that great things lie ahead.

- [ ] **Think about the very big picture.** This is one meeting. It's one of thousands of meetings you'll have in your career. It's important, yes, but it's still just a meeting. Ultimately, this meeting is about people getting to know each other. This organization has invited you here to better understand who you are. You've accepted the invitation because you wish to know more about this organization, this position, and these people. That's really it.

- [ ] **Congratulate yourself on being in this place.** Feel good about what you've done to earn this interview.

- [ ] **Congratulate yourself on your career so far.** You've experienced and achieved incredible things. More interesting projects and meaningful experiences lie ahead. Like all professionals, you're an accomplished person on a career journey.

- [ ] **Think positively about the upcoming meeting.** People react to positive people with more positivity. Smile. Maintain good eye contact. Look for reasons to truly enjoy this experience.

And be yourself. Your optimistic, gracious, well-meaning self.

Good luck!

Post-interview Debrief

THE QUESTIONS:

What questions did the interviewer(s) ask?

____

____

____

____

____

____

How did you feel about the questions? Did they seem easy or difficult? Were they typical questions (or surprises)?

____

____

____

____

____

Did you answer all the questions? Why or why not?

____

____

____

THE REACTIONS:

Overall, how do you feel about the interview?
What's your gut reaction?

Which answers seemed to draw a response from your interviewers? What responses did you notice?

Was there any personal connection?
Laughter? Shared interests?

Did any of your responses not go well (you drew a blank, got offtrack, forgot key information, etc.)?

Follow up within 24 hours

Have the correct names and titles of everyone you met with. Send a unique written note to each person.

- [ ] ______________________________
- [ ] ______________________________
- [ ] ______________________________
- [ ] ______________________________
- [ ] ______________________________
- [ ] ______________________________

Include these in your follow-up:

- A thank-you for the opportunity to meet
- A recap of areas where you fit the position best
- A brief response to any of the questions you didn't answer well

AFTER YOU FOLLOW UP, REFLECT ON THESE POINTS:

What did you do really well? (Congratulate yourself!)

What will you do differently next time?
(Okay. You learned something valuable!)

What are you still unsure of?
(Who could you ask about this?)

Decide to keep what will serve you and let go of anything that won't!

NOW IT'S *YOUR* PART

GO GET THAT JOB!

Also by Marcia Ballinger, PhD and Nathan A. Perez

The 20-Minute Networking Meeting

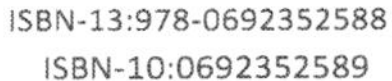
ISBN-13:978-0692352588
ISBN-10:0692352589

ISBN-10: 0-9859106-4-X
ISBN-13: 978-0-9859106-4-8

ISBN-13: 978-0985910600
ISBN-10: 0985910607

"*The 20-Minute Networking Meeting* does a great job spelling out highly effective strategies for building, expanding, and working with your network. This book offers valuable insights for honing your networking skills, whether you're a recent graduate or a seasoned veteran with 25 years in the workforce."

—JOHN A. CHALLENGER, CEO, Challenger, Gray & Christmas, Inc.

"I wish I had read this book before I started my networking. When I think of all the classic mistakes that I made—mistakes that are clearly outlined here—I'm embarrassed that I wasted time being less effective than I could have been."

—LAURA LIU, former Senior VP International, Northwest Airlines

"I couldn't put the book down once I'd started. A topic often talked about, but not addressed directly for executives. While I've considered myself a good networker, this book will give me the tools to be a great one."

**—LINDA THRASHER, former VP of Public Affairs,
The Mosaic Company**

"An excellent read. Many leaders waste valuable networking meetings, but *The 20-Minute Networking Meeting* demonstrates how to avoid this pitfall by illustrating what effecting networking is, forcing you to look in the mirror while motivating you to improve your skills."

—MARK DALRYMPLE, retired President of Schwan's Consumer Brands

"If you're in transition, you need this book. If you're working, you need this book. If you're living in a connected world, you need this book. I recommend this to emerging workers, folks in established jobs, people in transition and retired people entering a new phase of life. It works for everyone."

—CYNDI LESHER, former CEO Northern States Power, an Xcel Energy Company

Praise for *The 20-Minute Networking Meeting*

★★★★★ ▾ 76

"I was blown away..."

"A Godsend..."

"Had a profound impact on the quality and outcome of my networking meetings..."

WHICH EDITION IS FOR YOU?

- **Graduate Edition —** for any job-seeking grad, whether continuing education, 2-year, 4-year, trade school, graduate, or doctoral level.
- **Professional Edition —** for job-seekers from any background—field sales to customer service; doctor to bartender; teacher to derrickman; legal aid to construction; plus retail and service.
- **Executive Edition —** for any job seeker with 10+ years of executive experience.

Available from Career Innovations Press.
www.20mnm.com

PHOTO BY JOSHUA OLSON PHOTO

Marcia Ballinger is Co-Founder of Ballinger|Leafblad, a Saint Paul-based executive search firm. With over 20 years in the executive search industry, she has conducted leadership search engagements in all industries and functions. Marcia is a frequent presenter to groups of professionals on the topics of career transition and job search strategies. She has been named a "Top Woman in Business" by the Minneapolis-St. Paul Business Journal, a "Real Power 50" by Minnesota Business Magazine and "50 Over 50" by AARP Minnesota. Marcia is the author of *The 20-Minute Networking Meeting.*

Kevin Johnson is Vice President of Client Relationships at Career Partners International, Twin Cities and bestselling author or co-author of more than 60 books.

Made in the USA
Lexington, KY
02 October 2018